Teaching Toddlers
the Bible

Teaching Toddlers the Bible

V. Gilbert Beers

VICTOR BOOKS
A DIVISION OF SCRIPTURE PRESS PUBLICATIONS INC.
USA CANADA ENGLAND

Copyediting: Lloyd Cory and Barbara Williams
Cover Design: Scott Rattray
Cover Photo: Bob Ebel

Library of Congress Cataloging-in-Publication Data

Beers, V. Gilbert (Victor Gilbert)
   Teaching toddlers the Bible / by V. Gilbert Beers.
     p.   cm.
   ISBN 1-56476-155-X
   1. Bible—Children's use. 2. Preschool children—
Religious life.
I. Title.
BS618.B44 1993
268'.432—dc20   93-19696
                                                CIP

2 3 4 5 6 7 8 9 10 Printing/Year 97 96 95 94 93

Contents

Preface

What This Book Is—and What It Is Not

God has a royal blueprint for your Toddler's personal and spiritual development, and He has appointed you as the general contractor to see that His blueprint becomes reality in your Toddler's life. He has appointed you as His personal representative—overseeing the interests of the King of kings, the Lord of life, the Creator of the universe in this vital endeavor. He has made you His ambassador to represent His interests in the life of a child, your child, but also His child.

And you thought you were merely the parent of a little kid!

What your Toddler becomes will largely be the fruit of your careful efforts as a parent. Some children wander from their parents' Christian world, of course. And some accept Christ and live His ways despite a lack of parental help.

But the norm is for children to reap the fruit from the seeds sown by their parents. Sometimes, as the Scripture tells us, this reaping goes on to the third and fourth generations. The reaping may be the fruits of godliness or corruption. Much of that depends on the type of seeds sown, or the seeds we neglected to sow.

This book does not give you six easy recipes for teaching your Toddler the Bible. It does not offer twelve "TV dinner-type programs" which when heated and served will do it all. Life is just not that simple, though some books try to portray it that way.

This is a construction manual of sorts, a guidebook for those who guide the life-building program of their Toddlers, a challenge to those parental guides of Toddlers, a shepherd's manual for parental shepherds of Toddlers. It deals with God's wonderful plan for a Toddler in the growing-up process and how we as parents and teachers, especially parents, may guide our Toddler through this growing-up experience with the Bible as his or her ultimate guide.

My philosophy of learning is that we parents, through times of delight with the Bible, Bible stories, Bible music and singing, and other materials about the Bible, (1) help sow the seeds of belief which will ultimately, through the growing-up years, mature in our child a Christian belief system or Christian worldview; and (2) through this belief system, the Bible will shape the character of our child (what the child is), distinguishable as Christian through the values or character traits learned from the Bible; and (3) this Christian character will live itself out as conduct, or what the child does. Because I am a Christian with certain Christian character traits or values, I will or will not do certain things. This is predetermined conduct, shaped in character, molded by belief which has come from the truths of God's Word.

I truly believe that our times with the Word must be times of delight. Heavy, unhappy, guilt-ridden times with the Bible are counterproductive. If we delight in His Word, we should delight in our times with the Word and in living out our Christian lives.

Teaching Toddlers the Bible may more properly be called helping Toddlers learn the Bible. Teaching happens when we help learners learn. Teaching Toddlers the Bible is actually shaping Toddlers' lives through Bible learning. At its best, it is a time of joy in the context of the most delightful period of life — early childhood. And you, the parent, have the most wonderful opportunity to shepherd your Toddler through the Toddler years, sowing seeds of Bible learning to prepare him or her for the next wonderful period of life and the Bible learning needed there.

Chapter One
What Do I Want My Toddler to Become?

Are you a person who supervises people? Perhaps you are a manager or executive. Perhaps you are a teacher or superintendent in a school system. Whatever you do to earn a living, you may be called on to set goals or objectives — for this next year, or for a longer period of time.

As I write this book, part of my work is to write goals or objectives each year for Scripture Press, to determine what we want to accomplish corporately by the end of the year, in our case the end of the fiscal year. I have been in several goal-oriented situations throughout the years, both in business and in education.

We who write goals understand that they are "stakes driven out there," or milestones, which we hope to reach. They are specific accomplishments we expect to happen, periodically and ultimately, as the fruit of our labor. But if we do not express clearly what we want to accomplish, how can we hope to accomplish it? If we do not establish milestones on our journey, how can we hope to reach them or know when we reach them?

Have you ever written down on paper your goals for each of your children? What do you want each child to become? If you could write a profile of your Toddler when he or she is grown and is ready to leave for college, the end product of your first eighteen years of hard work, what would it be? By the way, you're never through parenting, even after eighteen years, but this is a dramatic milestone on your child's journey.

I have done this. But candidly, I wrote these goals after my unwritten goals were accomplished. I wish I had expressed these, at least to myself, when each of our children was a Toddler. What I have written may help you in setting goals for your Toddler. These goals have been accomplished in my grown children, but I have already confessed that I wrote them after the fact. Now they are goals for my grandchildren.

1. I want my children to become Christians, to accept Jesus Christ as Savior.

2. I want my children to form a strong Christian belief system—a "Christian worldview" or "Christian life view." This is a consistent system of beliefs that distinguishes them as Christians.

3. I want my children to grow to be strong Christians, that is, to develop strong character that is clearly Christian character.

4. I want my children to conduct themselves as Christians should live. This means living out their Christian character which personifies their strong, unique Christian beliefs.

Let's stop here for a moment. These are the four foundation stones in the process of building lives, whether you are a parent or teacher. Your ultimate goal, as mine, is not to teach the Bible as fact only, or even as truth only, but to help children of all ages, starting with the Toddler age, to learn the Bible so that they will become Christians, establish a Christian life view and belief system, apply truth to shape character, and thence affect their conduct. The next two chapters will spell out these four life-building processes more, as well as the specific goals that can flow from them.

I hope you read the Preface of this book. Even if you did, I want to remind you again that this book is not about six easy ways to teach the Bible to Toddlers. It is about the whole process of building your child's life, starting now at the Toddler age, through Bible reading and Bible study. This is not a book of gimmicks or methods, but a book about a wonderful process that has worked in our family. It is partly testimonial, partly educational, partly inspirational and motivational, and partly just plain good sense that works.

This wonderful process is about childhood, and growing up, and how the Bible impacts the growing-up years. It is about parenting, that most wonderful, high and holy opportunity and privilege, of guiding a child through each stage of that growing-up process, starting now at the Toddler age.

Chapter Two
Specific Goals for My Toddler

Let's build now on those four vital foundation stones laid in chapter 1. Here are some specific goals which I would have for my child if I had a new baby today. Since my children are all grown, I hope these will apply to my grandchildren. You may wish to adopt these as your goals for your child, starting now at the Toddler age. If you are a grandparent or a teacher, you may share them with a parent you know and encourage that parent to set goals for his or her own children.

As parents, our goals are different from corporate and educational goals. We are shepherds or guides, not managers or executives, in our child's life. We do not pull or push our children toward goals, but guide them, encourage them, help them learn, lead them, love them, and pray them toward the goals.

As a Toddler matures into an older child, perhaps you can share some of these goals, or find life-building materials which incorporate these goals, so that your child can "buy into" them, and thus set them as his or her own life goals.

1. I want my children to love the Bible, God's Word, and read from it daily, learning its life-changing truths, applying them to their lives, and becoming godly people by applying that truth to their character.

2. I want my children to live God's way as they prac-

tice God's truth at work in their character. As they walk with God, their footprints will then lead others to Him.

3. I want my children to exemplify those values that are at the heart of Bible truth, such things as honesty, truthfulness, kindness, generosity, compassion, loyalty, and so on. More will be said about values throughout this book.

4. I want my children to share God's Word and His ways with others through verbal witnessing and role-modeling.

5. I want my children to marry Christians and to cultivate the practice of the presence of the Lord in their wider family.

6. I want my children to exemplify godliness in their chosen work, and as they do it with excellence, they will also do it as good servants of the Lord.

7. I want my children to put their families first, after God of course, and not let their jobs or anything else cause them to neglect this priority.

8. I want my children to serve God to the best of their abilities, to be good disciples and good leaders.

9. I want my children to be good stewards of the money and other resources that God gives them.

10. I want my children to manage their lives with discipline and not let mediocre things replace those things that should be in first place.

11. I want my children to be people of joy, to delight in God and His Word, to enjoy their families, and to delight in living lives pleasing to God.

12. I want my children to be sober in those things that deserve serious consideration, but to brighten life

with good humor, especially learning to laugh at themselves, so others will see that their inner joy finds outer expression.

13. I want my children, when they become parents, to lead their children into God's ways, through God's Word and with God's full approval.

Your goals may be similar, or quite different, but I would encourage you to set goals now. Remember, however, that your child will ultimately choose whether these goals are accomplished. You and I do not control a child's life, but gently lead him or her toward goals. Your work during your child's Toddler years will leave lasting effects. Your personal investment in your Toddler will leave eternal footprints on that VIP's life.

Chapter Three
How the Fabric of Life Is Woven

So I am a new parent and I'm holding my beautiful new baby in my arms. I plan to feed her, bathe her, brush her hair, and teach her to brush her teeth. I will wash his clothes, toilet-train him, and teach him to eat. Isn't this enough?

So far we've dealt with physical needs. Think of the social, mental, and spiritual dimensions of your child's life. It is not the purpose of this book to help you train your child physically, socially, and mentally. Much good material has been written on these subjects. It is the purpose of this book to help you develop your child spiritually through your use of the Bible. Spiritual development will impact mental, social, and physical development. It will help your child be a better-adjusted child in all facets of life.

This book focuses on your Toddler and the Bible. It focuses on developing your child's belief system, which shapes Christian character, which finds its expression in Christian conduct. There is a temptation in some books and systems to leap from the Bible to conduct. I truly do not believe it works that way. When we accept a truth from God's Word, we weave it into our belief system (Christian worldview or Christian life view). Our belief system is the "software program," to use computer terminology, from which Christian character is shaped. As we believe, so we become. Then Christian character works its way out into our hands and feet and lips — our conduct. As we are, so we shall do. Through our beliefs we become different people (our character). Through our character, who we truly are, we do certain things (our conduct).

Belief, character, and conduct must all be in sync. If I truly believe that I should be honest, I will become an honest person. My character accepts the fact that all of my future conduct will reveal an honest heart and mind.

But if I go that far, and act dishonestly, I am at odds with myself. I am out of sync. I will not be happy. There are a lot of unhappy Christians out there who have allowed their conduct to get out of sync with their belief system and their character. What they practice is at odds with what they preach. This breeds unhappiness — a discordant spirit within us. So belief, character, and conduct must harmonize. Otherwise life is out of harmony.

As parents, our role is to help our Toddlers BEGIN to learn what they believe. Our role is also to help them BEGIN to weave this belief into their little lives and shape who they become. THEN they are ready to see conduct that harmonizes.

Childhood is that wonderful growing-up experience, during which God has planned for a child to mature step by step. At each step the child is able to absorb a little bit more than at the previous step. Not only that, but as we will discuss in the next chapter, God planned for childhood to be a process of delight. Childhood at its best is something of a fairyland, a wonderful time of interacting with the Creator's wonderful world; the Creator's appointed guide, the parent; and the delights of parent-child relationships.

Does this really work? Yes, I can testify that it worked in each of our five children. It really does!

Our society has moved away from God's wonderful plan. It has distorted the parental role, cast a cloud over Christian values and beliefs, undermined character, and revealed unwholesome conduct as not only the norm, but the desirable norm. The Christian life-building system does not follow the track that society at large is following. You must choose for your home and family to do it God's way, the way He planned, rather than the way society does it.

If I communicate nothing else in this little book, I want to communicate to you the joy of being a faithful shepherd for your Toddler. I want to communicate that you will be a far happier person when you see your Toddler grow in God's way through the wonderful life-building system that He created for us.

Chapter Four

Childhood—God Had a Great Idea

The creation of Adam and Eve worked. Life could start as an adult. God proved His point in Eden. Adam and Eve, the only people who were never children, seemed to get along fine until the serpent messed up their lives. So why didn't God start all of us as adults?

Why bother with messy diapers, milk bottles, peanut butter and jam-smeared faces, runny noses, muddy clothes, wailing and whining, the 10,000 "no's," and all the other things that frustrate young parents? Why?

Why bother with the whole thing called childhood? Why not just start us all out as adults? Why not start out being productive? Why put us through all the agony of growing up and learning how to learn? Why put parents through the trouble of parenting? Why, Lord, why? Why not make it easier for everyone and start as adults?

Those of us who have been parents or grandparents, can answer that quickly. Who would want to miss the delights of childhood? Who indeed? God had a great idea in the way He planned it. He had a great idea called babies, and Toddlers, and childhood.

Please understand that I am not writing this from the psychology section of the library. I am writing this from forty years of being a *very* involved father of five and a *very* involved grandfather of eight. For twenty years I worked at home and was about as involved with my children as a mother would be. I count those years as my highest privilege in life. So when I praise childhood, I do it from the vantage point of a dad who has wiped runny noses, changed diapers, held bottles, washed peanut butter and jam faces, and still loved it.

There is a trend, possibly a movement, afoot today to shortcut childhood, to rob children of childhood. Get them going earlier on adult living. It is a trend that lets little children watch TV programs and movies beyond the capacity of their fragile hearts and minds. It puts bras on little girls, earrings on babies, and pressures little boys to do in athletics what their fathers wished they could have done, but didn't. It tosses problems and life-threatening situations at children that even adults find difficult to understand. It exposes little children to the ugly, corrupting side of sex before they can comprehend God's beautiful reason for making such a thing.

The Lost Childhood Syndrome, too large to deal with adequately in this book, is of such concern to parents and educators that it has prompted books in the general marketplace. Two books on the "must read" list have been around several years. The authors do not identify themselves as Christian. But they spell out the problems that should alarm us as parents and teachers. You may want to read Marie Winn's *Children without Childhood* and David Elkind's *The Hurried Child*.

Counselors tell me that unwholesome problems and practices that used to be identified with high school young people have slid down through junior high and even into grade school. Increasingly we read of children, young children, involved in crimes and ugly adult-like situations. Children are forced into adult roles. The big news story as I write this is about a suburban couple, living in a lovely home, who went on a nine-day vacation over Christmas, to a resort, leaving their nine-year-old and four-year-old daughters alone at home to cope by themselves. The little girls leaped over a lot of childhood during those nine days.

Of all people on earth, we who claim to be Christians must not take part in shortening or eliminating our children's God-given gift of childhood. Please! As a parent or teacher, your highest privilege, honor, and opportunity is to see that your children are awarded that most wonderful experience in life—childhood—and all of the wonders that should come with it.

God had a great idea when He planned for us all to walk step by step through the wonders of childhood. He planned these steps carefully and associated certain wonderful experiences and growing-up delights at each step. It's our job to make sure these things happen. It is also the most wonderful experience of any person's life to do this—if you make it so.

Chapter Five

Growing Up—What Adam and Eve Missed

I feel sorry for Adam and Eve. They had Eden. But they missed childhood. I would rather have had my childhood than Eden. It is more glorious. Adam and Eve missed God's plan for the rest of us—to grow step by step through a divinely crafted plan. And what a plan it is! God's finest creative genius came to a focus when He planned childhood.

I wouldn't want to be an infant all my life. Nor would I want to be a thirty-nine-year-old all my life, or a fifty-nine-year-old. I look back with delight at each stage of my life. Some brought more pain than others. Some brought more delight than others. But I value each one. I look back with delight at each stage of each of my children's lives. I wouldn't want to have missed one of them. Each was filled with great challenge, but with greater delight.

You and I are still "growing up," or should I say "maturing." We will continue to do that until the day we die. Then, if we are Christians, we will graduate into everlasting life on a much higher plane than we could now dream.

Five times my wife Arlie and I picked up our newborn infants and glowed. A little of her, a little of me, a great deal of God's creative genius. A life had begun and we were privileged to lead it through the growing-up years. My only regret is that I couldn't be there almost every hour with my growing-up children. But I was there for most of it and was deeply involved. What a privilege! What an opportunity! I would not trade that opportunity for all the gold in the world.

There was the first coo, when baby responded to our verbal vibes. It's enough to make a parent go into the ninth heaven. There were first steps, the first smile, the first time our child could sit up, stand up, and then take a few steps. There were "first things" in so many growing-up experiences, and each was a moment of profound delight.

But growing up is much more than physical, mental, and social development. This book will focus more on spiritual growth, especially during the Toddler years, and especially how that growth comes from God's wonderful Word.

Having spent many delightful hours with the thirteen Toddlers in my life, I am convinced that we start spiritual growth at birth, or even nine months before birth. As the child grows through each step, the Word should not only be our guide, but the child's guide, the child's source of learning about God—learning to love God, and learning what life is all about when we live God's way.

The joy of parenting comes to its full flower as we sing songs about Jesus, read stories from God's Word, point to God's creative genius in clouds and leaves and a thousand other delights of His world, introduce our growing child to God's house, and God's ways, and model for our growing child what it means to be a

Christian and what it means to grow in a Christian family.

The joy of grandparenting is seeing your grown children so delighted with what they received that they do it all over again with their growing children. Isn't that the way God intended? I think so.

The greatest joy of my life is seeing our grown children doing all of these things that Arlie and I considered so important as they grew. They are all Christians, all married to Christians, and all raising their children for the Lord. Our oldest son, Doug, graduated into heaven when he was twenty-six, snatched from us through an auto accident. What a relief to know that he was a Christian.

If this book can accomplish only one purpose, I would hope that it will encourage you to be involved through each step of your child's growth, and to involve the Bible, God's Holy Word, at each step. If I can accomplish one thing in this book, it would be to stir you to begin this process at birth, or possibly nine months before birth.

Nothing in life is more important than this. Nothing will bring you greater rewards. Nothing.

Chapter Six

The Delights of Childhood—Start Them Now

As I thought of all the things we did with our children, the things that made childhood what childhood should be, I had quite a catalog. I won't try to list them all in this little chapter, but only give you a sampling. These are the experiences through which you and I can heighten our children's awareness of our loving Lord and His wonderful ways, and how they can walk in God's ways. We can bring the Word softly into some of these experiences, and firmly into others.

Many of our times of childhood focused on creation. We caught butterflies with our children and started a collection. Each butterfly that we examined was a time to talk of God's work of beauty. Birds visited our bird feeder daily, if not hourly, and we had another opportunity to talk of the wonders of little bird hearts beating, how birds found their homes, and how God provided for these little creatures.

First snowflakes, or a walk in a winter woods, or frost on the window always brought forth some comment about our Creator. Not heavy, long-winded sermons about Him, but light, loving comments about His works of beauty. A sunrise, or sunset, or moonrise always sparked a time of God-consciousness, as did the clouds in the sky. Our grown children are all "cloud fans," lovers of the clouds, and I believe they always think of our wonderful Lord each time they see a thunderhead or an approaching storm or puffy white clouds with distinct animal shapes, because that's what we often talked about. Experiences with the wind reminded us of God's presence—a kite on a windy day, blowing dandelion seeds into the wind, blowing bubbles and watching the wind take them away, higher and higher.

Seasonal touches of God's creative work are fun childhood experiences. Picking apples or strawberries or cherries or some other fruit reminds us of God's loving provision. Pumpkins and oranges are seasonal signs, reminding us that God still manages the cycles of life. The autumn leaves, spring flowers, summer canoe rides—all brought little opportunities to quote a Bible verse or merely to drop a loving comment about the Lord.

Food always prompted brief prayers of thanksgiving. "Thank You, God, for our food" was our prayer for the Toddlers. Later, prayer became more detailed. Food was not always just at the dinner table, but sometimes a hot dog or hamburger on the move. But usually we stopped to thank God for giving it to us, reminding the child that all food comes ultimately from God.

Traditions, which we'll talk more about later, became reminders of God's goodness and His Word. Each Christmas Eve, through the years, I have read from Matthew 2 and Luke 2. It was always expected. No one ever argued about it. From birth, our children came to accept the real Christmas story as the story of Jesus at Bethlehem. We enjoyed all of the festivities and traditions that are Christmas, but at the heart of it all was God's plan for sending Jesus.

We often reminded our children that our house and car and clothing were gifts from God. He allowed us to work so we could earn the money to buy these things. Yes, we worked to get the money. But God gave us the strength and opportunity to do it.

One of the keys is growing up with a "God-consciousness," and a sensitivity to God's Word associates those little comments about God with times of gratitude and delight. The growing child learns that we are to delight ourselves in the Lord.

But they learn also that in times of trouble or difficulty, He is there to help them. So in those times we remind our children to reach out to God and ask for His help.

Delight in the Lord in times of joy. Seek the Lord and His help in times of trouble or pain. These lessons can be learned, even during the young Toddler years.

Look for little opportunities each day to stir the God-consciousness of your Toddler. God gives us food. He gives us other things. He is with us when we travel. He cares for us. He hears us when we pray. He takes care of us in scary places. He is there. He loves us. He wants to help us.

Chapter Seven

The Most Important Three Years of All

If someone asked you, "What are the most important three years of life?" what would you answer? My answer would come quickly, without hesitation, "The first three years."

Think of it. During those first three years, which in this book we call the Toddler years, we learn every basic in life.

Physically, we learn to respond to the world around us with our five senses. We learn to see the world around us with rapidly expanding sensitivity. The world God made unfolds before our eyes proportionately more during the Toddler years than in any other three years of our lives. The same is true of our hearing, our taste, our touch, our sense of smell. They are all cultivated more during those first three years than in any other three years.

By the age of three we can discern colors and shapes and sizes and textures. We know which flavors are vanilla, peppermint, chocolate, and orange. We learn what is soft and what is rough or hard. And we learn to appreciate the distinctions among these flavors, textures, and colors. We learn to like some and dislike others. We learn what is yucky and what is tasty, what is sweet and what is sour.

During these first three years we learn to eat, to begin

to take care of our body, and to manage our bodily functions through toilet training. We learn to wash and bathe and clean our teeth. We learn something about taking care of our appearance and our clothing.

Socially, we begin to learn how to respond to other people. We learn concepts such as kindness, love, gentleness, thankfulness, and a number of others that we put under the umbrella of values. We learn about family and parents and siblings and the wider family with uncles, grandparents, and cousins. We learn to play together and do some little chores together. Hopefully we learn to keep our rooms clean.

Mentally we learn many things. The mind of a Toddler grasps those concepts just named—colors, textures, shapes, sizes, flavors, and many others. The Toddler begins to learn ABCs and 1-2-3s. Letters and numbers emerge in the Toddler's unfolding world.

The Toddler learns to respond to the wonderful world that God made. He or she learns to appreciate the wonders of things around and to associate God the Creator with them.

Spiritually, the Toddler learns who God is, and some of the key qualities about God. The Toddler can learn to pray simple prayers and associate God or Jesus with events that happen in the family.

Since I developed *The Toddlers Bible,* I have heard some wonderful stories of the way Toddlers have responded. One lady wrote to say that her two-year-old takes "her Bible" to bed with her instead of her stuffed animal. Another spoke of his two-year-old walking around the house and saying things like, "My Bible,

Daddy. I'm going to take it to God's house with me."
Another couple, friends of ours, have triplets. They also
have copies of *The Toddlers Bible*. Their Bibles are iden-
tical, yet each triplet knows exactly which is his and
hers.

Is it too early to introduce the Bible to Toddlers? I
think it is never too early. Obviously an infant can't
memorize Bible verses or learn doctrines. But twos and
threes will amaze you with their ability to soak up Bible
stories, Bible people, Bible truths. Even an infant will
form vibes, growing-up vibes, of a parent, or parents,
reading the Bible.

These first three years are the years when children
learn to think of God with positive vibes, no vibes, or
negative vibes. During these three years children learn
those same attitudes toward the Bible. They learn most
of these attitudes from your attitudes. If you love the
Word and they see you read it and hear you share small
but delightful bits of the Word, they will form a positive
image of the Bible. A lifelong desire to read, understand,
and apply the Word of God can emerge during these
three years. A lifelong neglect of the Word can begin
here too. The way we present the Word to our Toddlers
can shape their attitudes for life.

Chapter Eight
How Much Can Toddlers Learn?

In many churches and Sunday Schools the department for twos and threes is called the Nursery Department. "Nursery" has a double meaning. In some situations, it means a place to leave children while an adult shops or goes about other activities. In church and Sunday School, that is an inadequate concept, merely a place to leave children while adults do their things. Hopefully the name implies a place for children to learn.

The term Toddlers, which in this book embraces the first three years of life, is a more active term. It implies that a child is doing something, going somewhere. We're not merely talking about baby-sitting, but action and learning.

There are differing ideas about learning at this age-level. One idea implies that little children up to three really are for baby-sitters, not teachers. At the other end, another view, which I hold, says that we have vastly shortchanged children this age and they can learn much more than we have tried to teach.

Having worked a lot at home with my thirteen Toddlers through the last forty years, I am convinced that Toddlers can learn much more during the Toddler years than most parents teach them. But parents must make a much more concerted effort to teach them or guide them in the learning process.

I fear for today's children, where we have designated the space in front of the TV as the nursery and the tube itself as the electronic baby-sitter. In an effort to get peace and quiet, it's so easy to stick a Toddler in front of the TV and know he will be glued to it for a while. For a short time when a mother must get something done, OK. But please be careful that this does not become a lifestyle.

We have already mentioned, in chapter 7, that a Toddler learns more before three than at any other comparable period in life. We discussed there the basics that a Toddler learns—physically, mentally, socially. But somehow when we get into spiritual things we wonder how much a Toddler can learn. I believe Toddlers can learn more than we have thought. They will if we help them. They can and will learn the Bible if we help them. They can learn many things if we parents will involve ourselves in helping to guide their learning opportunities.

I am not advocating a highly structured school process, but one that is delightful and casual, one that stirs the imagination and eagerness of a Toddler to learn. We can't pour tons of information into Toddlers and expect them to process it the way older children can. Also, certain types of information don't compute in a Toddler's mind. A two-year-old wouldn't do well in world geography. But many two-year-olds who are growing up in bilingual homes are learning two languages.

How much Bible can Toddlers learn? Toddlers using *The Toddlers Bible* are learning more than their parents expected. We are hearing this from parents. Parents are reporting back to us that their Toddlers are learning about key Bible people. They are learning Bible stories and some are becoming favorites. They are learning simple Bible concepts. One mother reported an incident in which her Toddler daughter, early age three, chided her parents for getting angry at her because she had learned in a story they read to her that people should control their anger. "Control your anger," she said. "That's what our story said."

The first step in learning the Bible is to learn to love the Bible. That is a basic purpose of *The Toddlers Bible.* It works. *The Toddlers Bible* puts the Bible at the Toddlers' age-level. We can't thrust an adult Bible at a Toddler and expect the child to love it. It's difficult for adults to do that. I believe delight in the Word paves the way for Toddlers to learn Bible knowledge. That's why *The Toddlers Bible* was developed the way it was, to stir the delight of Toddlers and cause them to say, "I love my Bible." Then they're ready to learn.

Chapter Nine
Some Ways That Toddlers Learn

Storytelling

Storytelling is certainly the first on the list. There is something in the telling of stories that captures the imagination of people of all ages. Jesus was a storyteller, and through His stories or parables, people learned about heaven and God and God's ways.

A good story has strong characters with strong qualities. We should learn moral and spiritual values by the way these characters respond to the problems they face. Courage or kindness or truthfulness or any of the great moral and spiritual values emerges as the story's characters wrestle with the problems they must solve. It is in the solving of a problem that a story is told.

Good stories for Toddlers have characters and plots, or problem-solving situations, to which Toddlers can relate. Toddlers must identify with the people and what they are trying to do. They must relate to their situations or settings.

Toddlers are ready for Bible stories if they are told at the Toddler's level and mind-set. They are also ready for stories about other Toddlers, as in *The Toddlers Bedtime Story Book*.

Start reading good stories at birth, or before birth. The level of comprehension grows rapidly through the Toddler years. Very young Toddlers may not understand all you read, but the sound of your voice, the pictures, the warmth of your presence, and the identification with characters will build vibes with Toddlers. Comprehension comes along with growth.

Music

I can still see Arlie sitting there singing nightly with our children, while they sat without a wiggle, making up her own melodies to many classic nursery rhymes, singing Bible-related songs. And today these grown children sing the same songs to their children.

The rhythm of songs, and the message buried deep in their lilt, may result in a strong learning process.

Games

One educational system has a game called the silence game. It encourages children to be as quiet as the birds outside. Do you think children will be more quiet playing that game, or responding to a shout to "Be quiet"?

Little games can encourage children to listen more, learn more, take part more, and delight in the whole process more. What kind of games can your Toddler play? You'll need to try different ones to discover what your own Toddler can do. There is a wide range of ability from age to age in the Toddler years, as well as from child to child.

Crafts and Activities

Don't expect your Toddler to have advanced motor skills. Those are developed later. Toddlers' works of art are crayon marks scrawled on a piece of paper. But if you have a Toddler in your house, you have discovered how much that child wants to help you in about everything you do, even things beyond that Toddler's ability.

Can a Toddler draw a picture of Jesus? Of course. But don't expect it to look much like a person, especially Jesus.

Should a Toddler make things? Yes, but you'll need to help each step of the way. In the doing, your Toddler will learn.

Keep some of your crafts and activities Bible-related. Make a Noah's ark. Let your Toddler help you. You'll probably do most of the work, but that's OK, isn't it?

Reading Pictures

This is a favorite with Toddlers. As you look at a simple picture, such as those in *The Toddlers Bible* and *The Toddlers Bedtime Story Book*, ask questions: Who is this? What is she doing? What would you do if you were there? What would you like to say to this person?

You are reading a story by reading pictures. Picture reading is a delight for Toddlers and older children as well.

Chapter Ten

Role-Modeling — What You Do Speaks Louder than What You Say

If I had to choose one method above all others for parents to teach Toddlers the Bible, I would probably choose role-modeling. What you do speaks louder than what you say, even to your Toddlers. If you preach one doctrine but practice another, your practice will nullify your preaching. That's true of all of us in all our relationships with each other, isn't it? But I think it is even more true of the children who watch us daily.

Toddlers are not ready for a structured course in doctrine. They will not associate chains of information over a period of time. Nor will they assemble a network of information that comprises a whole system. But they will absorb bits and pieces which begin to form their early stages of a whole life view.

If that is true, should we try at this age to teach the pieces of the overall Christian life view? Yes. Because the little pieces are like seeds sown, and ultimately will grow and bear fruit in the whole structure of a Christian life view. You might call this a Christian Head Start program of sorts, getting a head start on a system of Christian beliefs which will make sense later as a whole system. It's never too early to start planting those seeds. As mentioned earlier, it's not even too early to start vibes prenatally. Unborn children will not "learn" as we think of learning, but I believe that something special happens as we sing or talk to our unborn child.

Role-modeling is practicing those doctrines which we verbalize, even the doctrinal seeds. A parent's role-modeling is a little child's first course in doctrine.

Suppose we tell our Toddler that God will listen to you whenever you pray. But we are too absorbed in our newspaper or feverish activity and a little too often say to our Toddler, "I can't talk to you now." How can a Toddler learn that God, whom he or she cannot see, will listen, when a parent who is there and is seen, cannot listen? Or suppose we tell our Toddler that God is always there. But we're seldom there. Or if we say that God is love and loving, but we are too often unloving or unlovely in our relationships with our Toddler, what is that child to think?

We parents and grandparents should make a conscious effort to role-model the simple doctrinal seeds we want to sow in the lives of our Toddlers. Let's think of a few here: God loves you (so do I); God is with you (so am I whenever I can be); God will never run away from you (neither will I); God takes care of you (so do I); God wants to help you (so do I); God listens to you (so will I); God forgives you when you ask (so will I); God's Word will tell you about Him (so will I); and so on.

Not only should we seek to role-model simple doctrines such as these, but also simple values. When we teach Toddlers forgiveness, do we practice it? Do we practice before our Toddler the other values we teach, such as truthfulness, kindness, generosity, love, patience, fairness, loyalty, goodness, prayerfulness, and gentleness? Do we practice these things in our conduct with our Toddler? Do we practice these things in our conduct with our mate, which our Toddler observes? Do we practice these things in our conduct with others—wider family circle, friends, neighbors?

Toddlers pick up vibes of our practice from our conversation. Do we speak hatefully of people at the dinner table, then talk about loving each other? Do we condone dishonesty or untruthfulness, even in another person, while we encourage our Toddler to be honest or truthful?

They will become like you. You may not think that's true today. But someday you will likely see your values, your attitudes, and your doctrines reflected in your children. Occasionally they may choose to reject the whole system you espoused. But more likely they will accept your doctrines and lifestyle in whole or in part. If your Christian life view is role-modeled in your life, it is more likely that your child will accept it as his or her own. What joy for a Christian parent to see children not only accept their Savior and their Christian walk, but to then role-model them later to their own children.

Chapter Eleven

Building Blocks of Life —
Moral and Spiritual Values

The term "values" has emerged on the national scene. But there are different views about the meaning of the word.

Let's start with what it means to be a Christian and to live Christianly or biblically or godly. First, we will agree, a Christian is someone of any age who (1) has recognized the presence of his or her sin and the need to be cleansed of that sin; (2) has acknowledged that Jesus Christ, through His death and resurrection, has provided a way for us to be forgiven and wants to forgive us; (3) confesses that sin to Christ, turns from sin, and asks for forgiveness and a new life in Him; and (4) desires to walk with Christ as a Christian (to live Christianly, godly, or biblically). You might play with the words, but the idea is there.

Walking with God or living God's way (living Christianly, godly, or biblically) is (1) letting the life-changing truths of God's Word change our character or personhood, and then (2) letting that changed character shape our conduct.

Life-changing Bible truths are truths in God's Word that will change our lives, help us live more biblically, or Christlike, or godly. The more we appropriate and apply those truths, the more we should expect our conduct to be Christlike.

Sometimes we call these Bible truths "Bible doctrines," because they are the doctrines (teachings) which will make us, after we have accepted Jesus Christ as our Savior and have determined to live the Christian life, a practicing Christian. We live out those truths which have shaped our character.

So what is the difference between a Bible doctrine, or truth, and a moral and spiritual value? A Bible doctrine, or truth, is God's teaching from the Bible. An example of a Bible truth from 1 John 4:7: As God loved us, so we should love each other. This is a specific doctrine or truth from God. An example of a moral and spiritual value: Love others. Moral, decent people, even if they are not Christians, recognize that they should show love to each other, be kind to each other, be honest with each other, and be fair with each other. They may not recognize that these are God's teachings, but they know these values are good. These are good moral values, marks of good, decent character. They come from God, through the Bible, but your non-Christian neighbors might not recognize that. They recognize these as wholesome, moral values, or character traits, which are marks of a good person.

Christians, on the other hand, with spiritual insight, recognize that these are more than just good moral values. They recognize these truths first as Bible truths, doctrines or teachings from God through His Word. Christians see the bigger picture, that moral and spiritual values are the character traits or marks of good character that come from Bible doctrine, God's teachings in His Holy Word. These character traits are expectations

45

of Christian character and conduct. We expect Christians to exhibit these traits and live accordingly. Call it godly living, living Christianly, being Christlike, or living biblically. It is all the same — letting the truths of God's Word, or doctrines, shape our Christian life view, which shapes our Christian character with certain distinguishable marks or traits, which then work their way into our lifestyle as Christian conduct.

It all starts with the Word of God. That's why we want to teach Toddlers the Bible, starting them with doctrinal "seeds," little seeds of God's truths which will grow as they mature. These little seeds, though very small, are there and later your children will allow them to grow in their lives. But let's not miss the tiny seed-planting of doctrines or values at this age-level. This may be called prelearning learning.

We will talk more about pre-learning learning in the next chapter. It's a phrase I have coined. Though someone out there may have used it before, I haven't seen it. But it embraces a concept I think is enormously important in helping our wonderful Toddlers learn the Bible.

Chapter Twelve
Pre-learning Learning

When does a child start to learn? Your wonderful new baby starts to learn something on the day of birth. An infant isn't ready for Bible doctrines or values, of course. But some of these are communicated through "vibes," the warmth of one's presence and personal involvement.

Too often we think of learning as cognitive, with the end result some recognizable fact or truth transmitted from a teacher to a student. That is a limited view of learning. Do you remember in chapter 7 all the wonderful things a very young child learns before the age of three? We would be hard-pressed to put many of these into the "cognitive" basket.

Are learning to talk, walk, eat, control bodily functions, and drink from a cup cognitive? These functions are learned. But they are not exactly part of a curriculum. We don't have a course for the Toddler on twelve steps to toilet training. We might have these twelve steps for a parent to use with the Toddler, but not for the Toddler directly.

Learning to talk fits us for a lifetime of dialogue with others. As a Toddler we learn the most basic steps of a life skill. Learning to eat fits us for social graces and later fine dining. But a Toddler is content to learn to get more of the stuff in his or her mouth than on the bib.

Many things a Toddler learns are a basic start for an ever-widening circle of learning in that skill or interest.

This is even more true in things like values. The smallest seeds are sown. It's difficult to say that a Toddler has "learned" that God loves her, that she should share with her brother, or that he should be kind to his sister.

Pre-learning learning sows tiny seeds. The seeds mature through the later years. Later we will list some of the values and doctrines which may be sown in tiny seeds during the Toddler years. This doesn't mean we hope to get the whole concept across, just the little seed, the pre-learning learning.

Some parents who use *The Toddlers Bible* tell me that the seeds are being sown through Bible people, Bible places, Bible stories or events, and Bible lifestyles.

Two-year-olds recognize Noah when they see the ark. They recognize Samson when they see the lion he wrestled. They recognize objects of daily living. They are not ready to comprehend the full story of obedience in Noah's life or moral weakness in Samson's life. Those lessons will come later. But they are responding to the "Bible seeds" being sown.

Should we withhold crayons from two-year-olds because they can't color within the lines? Of course not. Be content with squiggly lines that have no recognizable shape. But your Toddler is using crayons, "drawing pictures," and having fun. Not only that, but if your Toddler has an older sister or brother, he is doing what the older sibling is doing.

Nor should we withhold stories or doctrines or values which are generally beyond the cognitive level of the

Toddler as long as we do not set unrealistic expectations in what the Toddler can learn. Much learning at this age is pre-learning learning.

I have wondered why our children, and many other children, have responded to the classic nursery rhymes, since many of them defy logic. It seems that the rhythm, the rhyme, the lilt, and the cadence transcend the logic. These things are also pre-learning learning, for they cast a rhythmic mold for learning to take place later. Logic can wait. The musical qualities of rhythm and rhyme can't wait. If we hold out until a child is old enough to deal with the logic, or lack of it, in nursery rhymes, we have waited too long. Millions of nursery-rhyme-loving children, now adults, will testify to that. Neither can we wait for pre-learning learning of Bible truths and values.

Chapter Thirteen

Learning Is More than Teaching

Teaching doesn't always result in learning. Learning doesn't always start with teaching. Sometimes we assume that because we teach, our learners learn. And we also often assume that all learning comes from teaching. Teachers teach and learners learn and they don't necessarily meet. Hopefully they do, but not always.

I hope people learn something every time I teach. But I'll accept the fact that some don't. Also I learn many things without a teacher. So do you.

The title of this book should really be *Helping Toddlers Learn the Bible.* But we don't have space on the cover to explain what that means. So I took the easy road, the one that doesn't require a lot of explanation.

Your role as a parent is to teach your Toddler many things. But you will find, if you haven't already, that your teaching is usually "helping your Toddlers learn" rather than didactic teaching in the traditional sense.

This is especially true at the very young ages. Toddlers are like little sponges, soaking up learning everywhere. Our primary job is to help them in their learning process.

My oldest daughter Kathy learned the alphabet when she was two. I didn't teach it to her. As I typed, at that time on an old manual typewriter, she would point at a letter and say, "What's that?" She *learned* the alphabet without one conscious effort on my part to teach her. I suppose you could argue that each time I answered her questions I taught. But she initiated the learning process. I didn't.

You will find this type of learning hundreds of times during the Toddler years. And in your frustration to "get something done" you may be tempted to leap over this grand opportunity for your Toddler to learn without your structured teaching program. Toddlers don't always choose the best times to ask their learning questions. You may be at your busiest when an all-important question comes up. You will need to decide on priorities at that time. Is it more important to get dinner finished on time or to take an extra minute or two and respond to a learning opportunity?

Sometimes we can plant seeds that stimulate learning questions. Good children's books plant seeds, stir the child to ask questions, and want to know more. "Why does that man look so sad, Mommy?" You now can help the child learn that Peter lied about Jesus. Lying made Peter sad. It makes us sad too.

Little walks together, trips together, going to the store together, almost anything done together will raise these little learning questions. You may be tempted to look on them as interruptions. Actually they are golden opportunities for your child to learn.

I heard of a Sunday School teacher who came prepared to teach "the lesson." Before she started, a little girl said, "My grandpa died this week. Teacher, what does it mean to die?"

The teacher was flustered and quickly said, "We don't

have time to talk about that this morning because we must get to the lesson." She was so preoccupied with teaching that she missed her glorious opportunity to spark learning. And what a setting for at least that child to learn more about life and death.

Each day look for those little windows of opportunity for your child to learn the Bible. You may teach it, or you may help the Toddler learn. It doesn't matter.

Plant seeds of learning by asking questions. Your Toddler may not have the answer, but your question may lead to a little talk in which you provide the answer. For example, you're walking with your Toddler and see a robin building a nest. "How does that robin know what to do?" you might ask. Your Toddler may say, "God helps it." Then you have an opportunity to talk a little about the way God plans for His creatures to take care of themselves. Not a long talk. Just a little. Plant a few learning seeds. You'll see the fruit of those seeds appear many times in many ways.

Chapter Fourteen

Turn Off the Tube—
Turn On Your Child to Learning

Sometime ago I spoke to a public school class about writing. These children, fifth-graders I believe, seemed to have an eager desire to learn to write. Their teacher had been working with them on writing projects. So their interest was primed.

I had a bag filled with objects to underscore my talk. The first object I pulled out was a remote control device. "What does this do?" I asked. Everyone said, "It turns *on* the TV." Everyone.

"But it does something else," I said. "It will help you write. Without this, you will probably never be a good writer. What else does it do to help you be a good writer?" At first no one volunteered the answer. Then one child gingerly said, "Turn *off* the TV?"

We live in a wonderful world of technology. I'm glad for my computer and laser printer, fax machine, copy machine, modem, telephone, telephone answering machine, and certainly my car. Without these technological marvels, my work would be greatly impaired.

I'm even glad for a TV set and video. I like to watch the news and weather. Once in a while Arlie and I will watch a video. Having said all of that, I believe that the indiscriminate use of TV is without a doubt the greatest deterrent to creativity and learning. But discriminate use can aid learning. There are many fine science and history videos. I appreciate them. But the tube is filled mostly with violence, sex, trash, and anti-Christian innuendos. A steady diet of that will kill your child's creativity, imagination, and learning.

"You will probably never be a good writer unless you learn to turn off the TV," I told my class that day. Many of them moaned, as if to say, "Do we *really* have to give up our treasure?"

Not only does TV dampen our spirit to learn, imagine, and be creative, but runaway TV watching will keep parents and children from doing the 101 wonderful experiences in which learning takes place. Teaching Toddlers the Bible, or helping Toddlers learn the Bible, assumes that you will find time to spend with your Toddlers so that they may ask you the learning questions or so that you can plant the learning seeds to help them ask those learning questions.

Teaching and learning need two people—the learner and the teacher, the one helping the child to learn. It's difficult for a Toddler to learn on her own, especially Bible learning.

Turn off the tube. Take your wonderful Toddler on your lap. Cultivate times of talking together, singing together, reading together. These are the times when learning questions emerge.

The habit of good reading begins on the lap of a reading parent or in the presence of a reading teacher. Toddlers love books. Twos can identify books and what is in them. I remember vividly each evening watching Arlie, with children wrapped around her, reading or singing with animation from a good book. No wonder our children love books. Our son Ron is now a vice president of a book publishing company.

My mother read to me as I sat on her lap. I grew up on a post-Depression grain farm, so we could not afford children's books. So she read to me from the great poets—Longfellow, Lowell, Bryant, Whittier, and others.

If you want a good book on this subject, my favorite is still *Honey for a Child's Heart* by Gladys Hunt. It's been around a dozen years, at least, but is still a powerful presentation by a woman who read to her children and created a family of book lovers.

Of all the influences in our darkening society, I think I fear the influence of amoral TV producers as much as any. I have often said in talks, "You wouldn't think of inviting a gang of strangers into your home each night and telling them to do whatever they wish to your children. But all over our land parents are doing this through the TV screen. And the gang of strangers is corrupting their children bit by bit."

Turn off the tube. Turn on your child to learning, and especially to learning the Bible as you sit with your Toddler and a book such as *The Toddlers Bible*.

Chapter Fifteen
Turn On Your Life—
Turn On Your Child's Life

One compelling reason for limiting TV is role-modeling. If you don't watch a lot of questionable stuff on TV, your children will not have as much appetite for it. Peers may build some of their appetite for TV, but at the Toddler age, you are the most significant other in your child's life.

One of the first steps in teaching your Toddlers the Bible is to be sure you are engaged on a regular basis in Bible learning. A public school superintendent told me this morning in a phone conversation about a teacher in her school. It was near Christmastime and the teacher asked the class who Mary and Joseph were. Only two children from more than twenty knew. When I heard that, I wondered how many of their parents knew the answer.

If parents don't read the Bible and show a love for the Bible, where does the child get that love? Parents, read the Bible. Cultivate a love for the Word. Make it a vital part of your daily life. From the overflow of your love for the Word, you will help your Toddler learn the Bible.

Honestly, are you excited about your Bible reading and Bible study? Does the Bible turn you on? If not, you may have inadequate Bible study materials. Look for some materials that will help you turn on your life to the Word of God. When you do, you will also turn on your life to the Lord Himself.

Are you excited about the Lord? Are you excited about being a Christian? Is it a genuine joy to walk with the Lord daily? If not, how can your Toddler cultivate a true love for the Word?

The Toddlers Bible was developed to help Toddlers learn the Bible. It was developed also to help Toddlers learn to *love* the Bible, learn to delight in the Word. From reports we hear, it is working.

The wonderful by-product of this is the increased love for the Word by parents who use it with their children. As they see their children turned on to the Bible it helps them get turned on also. This is a switch. Usually it is the other way around. Parents are turned on to the Word first, then their children.

In what other ways are you "turning your life on" so that it may turn on your Toddler? Are you in the wrong job and this casts a shadow over your Bible study and your joy for Christian living? Perhaps you should try to change, even to a job that pays less money. Are you involved in the Lord's work in your church in a way that turns on your life? Are you reading the right books and magazines, or is your reading a downer? Are you associating with the right friends? Or are they downers? Are you enjoying some recreation and fun? Do you love to laugh, or have you forgotten how?

Without the joy of the Lord and the delight in His Word in your life you may not be turned on. And if you're not turned on, you may not turn on your Toddler to life and to the delights of the Word.

Draw a line from top to bottom on a piece of paper. At the head of one column write UPPERS. At the head of the other write DOWNERS. List those things you encounter in the course of a week which are uppers — things that turn you on to a more zestful living. How many Bible-related things are in the list? List those things in the other column which are downers. Are any Bible-related things there? If so, you need to change your materials, or your methods, or your timing, or something.

What does this have to do with teaching Toddlers the Bible? More than you may realize. Turn on your life for the Lord and His Word and watch your Toddler turn on also.

Don't you find it easier to gravitate toward Christians who are turned on to their Lord and the Bible? I'm not talking about a false glibness about spiritual things, but a true joy. Your own relationship to the Lord and to the Bible is a vital key to Bible learning in your home, whether it is teaching Toddlers, or children of any age, about the Bible.

Chapter Sixteen

The Second Dark Ages — Where's the Light?

Have you read about the Dark Ages? It was a grim time in the world's history. For the most part, the church gave up its light-giving and life-giving role. It became a politically motivated institution. The Word of God faded into the background and lost its impact on the average person in his walk on Main Street.

Not many today associate the Dark Ages with joy or happiness. Creativity and learning were obscured. Art and culture and reading for the masses were unimportant. So human dignity sank to a low.

I fear that we may be sinking into the second Dark Ages. I hope that I am wrong. I desperately hope that I am wrong. But I see dark clouds on the horizon. I am not alone. Many who watch the trends of the church and society in history have the same fears. There are quite a number of books written on the subject.

The gathering clouds that foreshadow another Dark Ages obscure the importance of the Bible, especially in the church and family. I see some flicker of hope among a few families and churches. But if you, like me, read surveys by the pollsters, you hear of a decreasing knowledge of the Word, and a decreasing commitment to its truths. Also there seems overall to be lacking a high view of the Scriptures which causes churches and families to hunger for its truths.

At no time in history have more Bibles been sold. At no time in history have more versions and variations been sold. Books about Bible study abound. Yet, despite this, those who work with college-bound young people are concerned about Bible illiteracy. We seem to be going through the motions, but are we really falling in love with the Word and allowing it to change our lives?

Would you not agree as you read the newspapers that we are in a darkening age in our society? Violence is at an all-time high, on the streets and on the tube. Perverted sex is at an all-time high, on the streets and on the tube. Perverted lifestyles, those that run counter to Christian lifestyles, are at an all-time high in both places. So is the drug culture. What we once considered a model family is no longer the norm in society and, in fact, we have to be careful if we project it as the norm.

As Christians we must speak softly about deviant lifestyles, lest we offend. Yet it is a national pastime on TV and in the media to ridicule Christians, Christian lifestyles, and Christian distinctives.

The hope of the world is in each generation, including our Toddlers of today, who will be the leaders of tomorrow. The hope for the world a generation from now is in the Toddlers of today, and the attitudes we help them build concerning the Word of God, the Bible learning we help them get, and how we help them apply the Bible to change their character and thence their conduct.

When we plead in this book for you to help your Toddlers learn the Bible, the impact is far more than merely one child growing up with a more delightful response to the Word. Collectively, our Toddlers of today will, a generation from now, make the difference in how our society and church shape the world.

If we can help today's Toddlers find joy in the Word, and help them apply it and appropriate it into their lives, they may well prevent that second Dark Ages which I fear is coming. A million of today's Toddlers turned on to the Word could make *the* difference in tomorrow's church and society.

That's why I invite you to join with me, there in your home, in turning your Toddler on to the Word. You may be helping shape the future of the world. That's worth doing, isn't it?

Chapter Seventeen

Bible Study Is for Real Live Persons

Have you ever read Dickens' book *Oliver Twist,* dramatized in the motion picture *Oliver?* If you have, you are reminded again that history records a sorry record of the way people care for children. Actually you don't need to go back into other chapters of history. Pick up today's newspaper and it is highly likely that there is at least one story of child abuse and child neglect. Some are horror stories.

While I am writing this book there are two stories that have caught the media's attention. I mentioned one earlier. According to news reports, a couple less than twenty miles from my home went on a nine-day trip to Acapulco over Christmas vacation. So far, so good. But news reports say they left their nine-year-old and four-year-old home alone during the nine days. The other story is about a little ten-year-old girl who was locked in a concrete vault under a garage for days because, according to news reports, she refused the advances of a neighbor man she befriended. The list could go on and on and on. Several stories have appeared lately of babies who have been shaken to death or beaten to death and even hanged.

Of course the most horrible story of all is the increasing national acceptance of the holocaust sweeping our land—killing unborn children. I came from a motel room one morning to see a car parked in the lot with two bumper stickers. One said PRO CHOICE. The other said SAVE THE BABY SEALS. We indeed have a national sickness when we show concern for baby seals but a total disregard for baby humans.

Are unborn babies humans? Are they really people? That's the issue today. Is an unborn child truly a person? If not, we're merely killing fetal tissue. If so, we're murdering a person. At which point does a person become a person?

I can tell you that during the pregnancies for each of our five children, Arlie and I had a profound awe for that little life developing in her womb. We prayed for that unnamed child. We talked to it and I'm sure Arlie sang to it many times. I say "it" because we had no way to know in those days whether that growing child was a he or a she. And we would welcome either with open arms.

A nation which takes a low view, or nonperson view, of the unborn child will also take a low view of the newly born (which leads to infanticide), or for that matter, children of all ages (which leads to child abuse). That nation's view of the aged follows closely—a dehumanizing view that leads to euthanasia. Spouse abuse is merely a symptom of a deeper cancer of the abandonment of personhood. If the other person, any other person, is not truly a person, it is tempting to abuse her, rape her, destroy her self-esteem, or view her as a sex object only.

Bible study is for real live persons. Before you absorb anything else in this book, you need to recognize that

Bible study is Person to person—from the heart of the person called God to the heart of the person who develops an eternal relationship with Him through the study of His Word. If we think of Bible study as a course in Bible knowledge only, we may as well study European history. If we think of Bible study as a study of doctrine only, we may as well study philosophical treatises.

Bible knowledge shares the historic and sociological and other contexts in which God's life-changing truth is set. Bible knowledge helps us understand the people and events in which, and through which, God articulated His truth. Bible doctrine is a systematic expression of those truths which God has given to change our lives. But ultimately Bible study is about the *Person* called God and His Son Jesus Christ. It is about His *personal* visit to earth as the Savior and His *personal* death on the cross for our sins, and about our need to *personally* accept Jesus Christ as our Savior and to walk His ways *personally*. Isn't prayer *person* to *Person* dialogue? Isn't witnessing a *person* to *person* sharing of our faith? Teaching Toddlers the Bible is therefore both Person to person (God's truth to the Toddler) and person to person (your personal help for the Toddler). It is also Person to person to person—God through you to your Toddler.

Chapter Eighteen
Your Toddler Is a Real Live Person

When the grand truth sweeps over you that your Toddler is a real live person, it will change the way you involve yourself in his life. When the grand truth lays hold of you that as a person, your Toddler, in God's eyes, is just as important as you, you will have a new view of how to build your Toddler's life.

Are you bigger than your Toddler? Yes. Do you have a more important role now than your Toddler? Yes, partly because you are God's appointed representative to help build that person's life.

Are you more important than your Toddler? As a person, God views us all equally—male or female, black or white, child or adult, baby or king.

Your Toddler is a real live person. That makes your Toddler a true VIP, a very important person. Anyone who abuses such a child is challenging God's very order for human growth. But please listen to this. Wonderful Christians are out there who would never abuse a Toddler. But some might neglect them—failing to follow God's order for their growth, and especially their growth through the Word of God. Jesus (Luke 17:2) deals with both—abuse and neglect—which causes one of these little ones to sin. Jesus had harsh words, that it would be better for a millstone to be tied around that person's neck and to be thrown into the sea. I didn't say this. Jesus did. I read neglect into this verse just as much as abuse.

As a real live person, your Toddler is on a growth track predetermined by God Himself. If a parent does nothing for a baby, that baby will, of course, die of neglect. If a parent feeds the child physically, but neglects the child spiritually or emotionally or mentally, the child's body will grow, but the child's personal life will be stunted.

Teaching Toddlers the Bible is much more than a course in Bible for Toddlers. It is helping your children (through the truths of the Word) grow in the pattern God planned for them. It is establishing a hotline between the personhood (heart and mind) of God and the personhood (heart and mind) of your Toddler. It is a form of networking, to put it in computer terminology.

The amount of time and energy you devote to teaching your Toddler the Bible will depend largely on what you think of God as a Person, what you think of your Toddler as a person, and how important you think it is for God the Person to impact your Toddler the person. Please read this paragraph several times and let its truth lay hold of you.

One more item to lay hold of. How much do you think the Bible will affect the place where your Toddler will eventually spend eternity? How much do you think the Bible will affect the entire life of your Toddler here on earth? If the life-changing truth of God's Word is so important, why then do we not spend more time and energy helping our children understand and accept it, *starting with the Toddler age?*

I have written dozens of books for children. There are hundreds of books, thousands of books, for children in print. But there are only a handful to help Toddlers know and love the Word of God. My passion to develop *The Toddlers Bible* was to give parents at last a Bible for Toddlers that they could truly learn to love. Not too much, not too little, just enough. From reports we are hearing, it is working.

Your Toddler is a real live person. God is a real live Person. You are a real live person. God wants you as a person to connect Him as a Person to your Toddler as a person. This is done through Bible study, the lifeline He established as *the* lifeline from His heart and mind to any other person's heart and mind, even the heart and mind of a Toddler.

This chapter is a plea to you as a parent to give your heart and soul to teaching your Toddler the Bible — not as information only, not even as doctrine only, but as the lifeline from the heart and mind of God as a Person to the heart and mind of your Toddler as a person.

Chapter Nineteen

Delight — The First Step in Bible Learning

If your child could draw well and would draw a picture of God, what would that picture be? Would God be smiling or frowning? Would He be an over-serious person, or a person with a twinkle?

If *you* drew a picture of God, what kind of picture would you draw? Would He be overly sober and serious, or a person of delight?

God is not a grumpy old man. He isn't a grumpy old woman either. God is not a person with a perpetual frown. He does not wear a mask of troubled seriousness.

Our God is a God who draws forth our delight. The Bible tells us so. For the sake of the many readers who use many different versions, the following are restatements of Bible verses (I'm not even trying to paraphrase, only to get the idea across to you here).

Deuteronomy 30: 9 tells us that the Lord will delight in us as He delighted in our ancestors.

Psalm 1:2 tells us that a godly person will delight in God's Word, the Law of the Lord.

Psalm 35:9 speaks of delight in the Lord and in the salvation He offers.

Psalm 37:4 tells us to delight in the Lord.

Psalm 43:4 speaks of God as my joy and delight.

Psalm 119, a long chapter, is a symphony of delight expressed to the Lord.

Before you try to stir delight for the Word of God in your Toddler, have you stirred that delight in the Word in your own life? If a friend described you to another friend, would he or she talk about you as a person who delights in the Word?

There is, of course, a sober or serious side to the issues of sin and salvation, Christian living, witnessing, and child care. It's a sober or serious matter because of eternal consequences.

But there should be a prevailing sense of joy and delight over all of our Christian experience. Bible reading, Bible study, and Bible application should all be times of delight. You and I, as parents or grandparents, should communicate our own personal delight in the Word as we cultivate a delight in the Word in that wonderful Toddler.

How can we make Bible reading or Bible study a time of delight? Don't associate a sense of guilt with Bible times. Are there occasions when you can't have your Bible time together? Don't lay a guilt trip on yourself or your children because of that. Are there occasions when Bible times don't work? Sometimes they bomb. Don't lay a guilt trip on yourself or your children. Laugh with them. Then try again.

I believe Bible times, or you may call them devotions, should be times of joy rather than pressure or guilt or somber tones. Otherwise a child grows up with Bible and delight on opposite sides of life's fences.

What are some ways to cultivate this sense of joy or delight? Here are a few simple suggestions: (1) Cultivate your own sense of delight in the Word first, so that it will "rub off" on your Toddler. Ask yourself frequently what specific delights you have received from God and His Word. (2) With young children, talk about God's good gifts. (3) Talk about ways God shows His love to you and your children. Bedtime can be a special time to read a Bible story, talk about God, and pray together. (4) Associate Bible times with happy times in your home, such as dinner, if it truly is a happy time. (5) Keep Bible time a happy time, avoiding conflicts at that time if possible. Think of other ways you can cultivate joy or delight at this time, then practice those ways each time you share a Bible time with your children of any age, but especially your Toddler.

Chapter Twenty

Can Toddlers Learn Bible Knowledge?

You may have the following books on your shelf of Bible study aids: a Bible dictionary, a concordance, a Bible handbook, a Bible atlas, and a commentary. All of these works, plus many other types, deal with Bible knowledge. These works deal with Bible people, Bible places, Bible words in your language or in the original languages, Bible topics, Bible history, Bible lifestyle, and so on.

Bible knowledge is a wide category, a catchall term for information relating to the Bible. Can Toddlers learn Bible knowledge? Yes, of course, but not all of the above.

Parents who use *The Toddlers Bible* tell me that their Toddlers learn about certain Bible people and objects associated with their lives. Noah and his ark are favorites. So are Samson and the lion. Can Toddlers learn about Bible people? Yes, they can. Can they give you character profiles? No, they can't. Can they give you the meaning of an original Greek word? Of course not. Can they get the idea of "please" and "thank you" and certain other words within their daily use, words that may arise in a Bible story or Bible-related story? Yes, absolutely.

In chapters 11 and 12 I spoke of seeds sown. In teaching Toddlers anything, including the Bible, we are sowing seeds of learning which will grow through succeeding years and ultimately bear fruit. Merely because a Toddler can't reap the full fruit of those seeds during his or her Toddler years does not mean we shouldn't sow the seeds.

I'll be content for my Toddler grandchildren to get acquainted with several Bible characters and some things they did. If seeds of doctrine or values are sown as well, and they are, that's wonderful. I'll be content also for my Toddler grandchildren to be exposed to a hundred of the great stories of the Bible, the events that formed the backbone of Bible history. Will they understand the context of that history? Probably not, until their late elementary or preteen years. But the seeds are sown.

I would like my Toddler grandchildren to learn that some Bible people, like Noah, were good people. I would like them to learn that Noah obeyed God, that he did what God wanted. I think they should learn that obeying God is something we should do too. They may not fully understand what that means, but they can learn that it's good to do.

I would like my Toddler grandchildren to learn what Noah did. He built a big boat called an ark. He did it because God told him to. We do many good things because God wants us to do them or parents want us to do them. Toddlers can learn that.

I would like my Toddler grandchildren to learn that some Bible people were bad people. I would like them to understand the difference between bad and good or evil and good.

In *The Toddlers Bible* parents introduce their Toddlers to Satan and his tempting ways. They see Jesus on the cross and learn why He was there. Will they understand the doctrine of redemption through the Crucifixion? Of course not. But the seeds are sown. The seeds of asking Jesus to be our Savior are sown.

In *The Toddlers Bible* parents introduce their Toddlers to God the Creator and His wonderful work as He made the world. Will Toddlers understand all about Creation? Even adults find it hard to fully understand. But the seeds are sown.

So much also depends on which side of the Toddler age your child is now. Are we talking about an infant? Don't expect much other than warm vibes and bonding. Are we talking about a child near three with a high IQ? You'll be blown away with how much that Toddler can learn. It also depends on how much time you spend with your Toddler to encourage learning.

Should we try to teach Toddlers Bible knowledge? Yes, as long as we keep realistic expectations and don't push the Toddler beyond his or her capacity to learn. Let your Toddler learn at his or her pace, not yours.

Bible knowledge is the framework in which Bible truth is cast. Yes, help your Toddler learn it at his or her pace. The seeds are sown. The fruit will be gathered later.

Chapter Twenty-one

Bible People—Role-Modeling in the Bible

Chapter 10 was about role-modeling, mostly your role-modeling as a parent. But there is another source of role-modeling, through Bible stories. Toddlers meet Bible people—good and bad. They see the good things they do and the bad things they do. They learn that good things others do are patterns for the good things they should do.

What do Bible people role-model for our Toddlers? Let's start with values. If you wanted your Toddler to learn kindness from a Bible person, which Bible persons would you think of first? Probably Ruth would come to your mind first. Here was a wonderful young lady who left her homeland to help care for her aging mother-in-law. You might also think of Dorcas, who in her kindness made good gifts for her neighbors.

What about courage? If you wanted your Toddler to think about a brave person, whom should he meet? How about Gideon, who fought a big army with his little band of 300? Or what about Queen Esther, who went before the king to beg for her people, even though she could have been killed for doing this?

Noah role-modeled obedience when he made the ark. Daniel role-modeled prayerfulness. He prayed when he knew he might die for it. Barnabas was a role model of a good friend, one who was willing to be a friend when it wasn't the easy thing to do.

Bible people also role-model doctrines, or Bible truths, at work in everyday life. If we looked for a Bible story that taught the Bible truth "God loves us," how would the Crucifixion story do?

Or if we wanted a story in which a Bible person role-modeled the Bible truth, "Jesus can do anything," how about the story of Jesus raising Lazarus or stilling the storm? Only Jesus, God's Son, can do those things. "God gives good food" can be seen in the story of manna in the wilderness. "God takes care of His people" is seen in the story of Baby Moses.

Bible people may also role-model a lifestyle—conduct that comes from godly character. When Paul was imprisoned at Philippi, he could have grumbled and cursed God. Instead, he praised God with songs. That's good role-modeling for people of any age, but I think a Toddler could get the idea of praising God, even when things aren't going well. Daniel role-modeled a lifestyle when he was captured and offered the king's food and wine. He refused what he knew he should not eat or drink.

A word of caution. Role-modeling from Bible people could lead us down the wrong track. When parents are role models to children they are living out the truths they "preach." In other words, they are the living embodiment of Bible truths which they are teaching. They are saying to their children, "When I share a Bible truth with you, I will first live that truth before you." This reinforces the instruction with role-model teaching.

But using Bible characters as role models is a little

different. A Bible character is not trying to teach your child a Bible truth. The person was living out a truth because he or she encountered a daily situation and responded God's way (or with a negative role model, *not* God's way).

Let's take David fighting Goliath as an example. Our temptation is to say to a child, "You should be brave because David was brave." But *both* David and Goliath were brave. The difference was that David faced a giant and Goliath faced a young man, *and* that David trusted God to help him and Goliath wanted no part of God. David won because he trusted God to help him, not merely because he was brave. David role-modeled bravery, but he was a much greater role model of trusting God to help him do the impossible.

Remember, we do not do something merely because someone else did it. David, for example, role-modeled a truth—God helps us when we trust Him, and may even do impossible things for us. That's a truth we should lay hold of to help make us different persons. Then we will be ready to trust God, not because David did it, but because we have accepted the truth that David exemplified.

Chapter Twenty-two

Theology at Two?
Can Toddlers Learn Doctrine?

Try throwing a heavy doctrine at a Toddler—predestination, for example—and watch her giggle or run away to play. No, Toddlers are not ready for a thick juicy steak of heavy doctrine such as predestination, at least not the term and the full-blown explanation given by theologians.

But there are simple doctrines which Toddlers can learn and should learn. Let me list a few, but certainly not all:

God made the world
God made you
God loves you and me
God gives us food
God gives us clothing
God gives us good gifts
God gives us His Word, the Bible
God is good
We should give to God
We should talk with God
We can't see God, but He sees us
God listens when we pray
Jesus loves us
Jesus died for us
We should please Jesus

We should tell friends about Jesus
Jesus can do anything
Jesus loves children

By the time Toddlers are three, they can know something about these doctrines, and many others. Will they know the full depth of each doctrine? Of course not. Do you fully understand God's love for you and me? But seeds are sown and a Toddler can begin to lay hold of very simple truths from God's Word.

The basic Bible truth for a Toddler is God-consciousness, a recognition that God is wherever we are and is a Person. Many adults today have not laid hold of this truth. This is the truth of truths on which all others are built. We can't accept truths about God's Word until we have accepted the truth that God is. Nor can we accept truths about God's qualities — those basic traits that are translated into values — until we recognize that God is God, that He is here.

Don't expect your Toddler to understand what a truth is and how truth works. That's difficult for us, isn't it? But a Toddler can recognize (understand may be too strong) that you want him to please you, can't he? She can begin to recognize that Jesus wants her to please Him, can't she? "Begin to recognize" means that the Toddler has early flickers of understanding, but not full understanding. But it is vital that these early flickers of understanding, or seeds sown, be planted in the hearts and minds of Toddlers.

Toddlers will also not likely follow a course of doctrinal study. You will. But the Toddler will not put all of the "beads" together in that chain of learning. So why follow a course of doctrinal study with young children? Because the child picks up the small bits of learning, even though he doesn't put it all together like beads on a string. You, the parent or teacher, see the sequence or overall plan.

I don't like to repeat myself too much, but sowing early seeds is still the best image. Yes, we should sow doctrinal seeds at the Toddler age, even though the Toddler doesn't really understand each one fully and can't put them together into a system.

There is another benefit of sowing these doctrinal seeds with your Toddler. As she grows, you have expressed Bible truths at the most simple stage. You are ready now to express them at a slightly more advanced stage. You are seeing God's truth in context to your growing child and you are better equipped to share that truth at the next stage of growth.

Chapter Twenty-three
Character-building Begins with the Bible

Ultimately when we speak of building lives, we must recognize that we are talking about building character. Character is what we *are*. Conduct is what we *do*. What we do comes from what we are. Conduct that is merely cloned from another is not character-driven. That kind of conduct is easily swayed by the wrong role model. Peer pressure, for example, drives many children to do things that they would never do if their actions or conduct was driven by character.

Why do some children buckle under peer pressure? One reason is that the wrongdoing is the *in* thing to do. That is, their peers are all doing it. If peers are all doing it, and they are driven by role-modeling or cloning only, they are ready to do this wrongdoing merely because their peers set the model (a bad model, but it is a model).

This is why Christian character-building is such a vital link in Bible learning. It is the fruit of our belief system, of the belief system of our children. As seeds of doctrine, or Bible truth, are sown in little lives, they begin to bear fruit. The child, little by little, begins to form a belief system. That belief system, if driven by learning the Word of God, becomes a biblical belief system, or Christian belief system. Sometimes we call this a Christian worldview or Christian life view.

It is this belief system then that shapes Christian character. As we settle on our Christian belief system and these beliefs become our convictions, we ourselves become what we believe.

Belief then becomes the engine that drives character. Character is the engine that drives conduct. The conduct of others, especially peers, should not become the engine to drive conduct.

When children mature in their Christian character, they predetermine what their conduct will be. A teenager, for example, is far less likely to engage in premarital sex if he has predetermined in his Christian character that this is not an option. It is not an option because he believes a Christian should not do this and that belief has settled what kind of person he is. The kind of person he is does not allow for this behavior or conduct.

All Christian belief begins with the Bible. Thus all Christian character is shaped by Bible truths or doctrines. Ultimately Christian conduct is Bible-based conduct. This is the reason why it is so vital for parents to begin a lifelong habit of Bible times with their children.

Keep expectations realistic, though. Unrealistic expectations set goals beyond the capacity of a child to accomplish. Will a Toddler have a full-blown belief system by the age of three? Of course not. We are all maturing in our belief system. A Toddler will have merely the first steps in a very basic belief system, little more than the seeds that have been planted.

A teenager who has matured through years of careful parental guidance through Bible teaching should have a belief system which has shaped his Christian character significantly. What a wonderful gift a parent can give to a growing child!

This process of developing a belief system which shapes Christian character, and then conduct, begins at birth and continues throughout the years at home. But in this book I want to stress the need to begin the process at birth and keep it going. Teaching Toddlers the Bible is therefore much more than teaching Bible knowledge which will accumulate through the years. It is also helping the Toddlers begin in a very small way that Christian system of belief that shapes character and then conduct.

Teaching Toddlers the Bible is the first step of leadership development. Young people who have grown up with parents who started their spiritual development as Toddlers, and continued it through the growing-up years, are much more qualified to assume leadership roles than those who have missed this process. Christian convictions and Christian character are the engines that drive a life of productive, creative work and ministry and offer the opportunity to do this in a leadership role.

Chapter Twenty-four

Bible Verses —
Where Do They Fit into the System?

Can Toddlers memorize Bible verses? How many can they learn? Which version should you use? What about a memory program? You and your friend may be on opposite sides of the fence on this one. There is an enormous amount of disagreement on Bible memory work.

First, there is the version issue. This divides many. Some feel the *King James Version* is the *only* version, not merely to memorize, but to use. They would argue that it is the only right version of the Bible. Others would say the *New International Version* is the right one. But then 35 million people have voted for *The Living Bible* by buying copies. That's not too shabby, is it? And of course we can add the *New King James, Moffatt's, Phillips,* the *New English, Berkeley, Goodspeed, Good News,* and many others. Which is right? That's for you to decide.

Then there is the issue of memorizing an entire verse or a portion of a verse. Many feel that a child should go for the whole thing, not a portion of a verse. That's quite a challenge for a Toddler. My guess is that you'll struggle with Bible memory if you expect twos and threes to memorize entire verses. I would settle for a portion of a verse that communicates a good message. Again, you must decide this for your child.

Many memory programs are packaged as a bunch of cards. That's also quite a challenge for twos and threes. To ease that situation, I wrote a book called *The ABC Beginners Bible Memory Book*. It puts memory work into the context of a story and gives choices of four versions.

I think we need to find ways to make Bible memory more fun, easier, and more to the point in a child's life. If you're not having much success with twos and threes in Bible memory, you may consider a change of methods. To start with, try memorizing portions of a Bible verse, rather than the entire verse. Don't set unrealistic expectations, or not much will happen.

Make memory work a game. Cut out pictures that remind the child of the verse and put them on the refrigerator or TV. Each time you open the fridge with your Toddler nearby, or each time you turn off the TV, say the verse and explain what it means. Example: Psalm 119:105 talks about God's Word as a lamp and a light. Cut out a picture of a light bulb or flashlight. Tape it in one of those places. Repeat the verse each time you use the fridge or TV. You'll be surprised to hear your Toddler start to repeat it, or at least part of it, when you least expect it.

Here's another one. Ephesians 6:1 tells children to obey their parents. You may find a picture of a parent and a child and put it in your Toddler's favorite book as a bookmark. Each time you read something from this book, look at the picture together and repeat the verse. You'll hear your Toddler repeat the verse or part of it at an unexpected time.

You can think of many other ways to put pictures and verses where your Toddlers will see them often—the door of your Toddler's room, on a favorite toy box, on your Toddler's bed, and so on. The object is to associate the picture and the verse, and to repeat it each time you encounter that object. After you have said the verse (please don't make it long) several times, you'll hear your Toddler begin to say pieces of it too.

Here are some tips to help Toddlers learn Bible verses: (1) Keep verses short or use portions of verses. (2) Associate a familiar picture with the verse. (3) Keep the verse (which your Toddler can't read, but you can), and the associated picture, near an object which you and your Toddler use together often (refrigerator, TV, favorite book, toy, game, and so on). (4) Don't try to memorize many verses. An occasional verse is better than a full-blown memory program at this age. Try different systems. Toddlers vary greatly in their ability to learn. (5) Make it fun. Don't make it a drag. Then watch the great rewards as Toddlers learn bits and pieces of the most wonderful Book in the world.

Chapter Twenty-five
Home Is More than a Toddler's House

There is a vast difference between a home and a house. "I'm going home," we say. Do we mean we're going back to our house, whether or not we have made it a home?

Home, in its full, rich Christian definition is that wonderful place where a Toddler begins a life of unique learning and where, guided by parents, he will grow biblically, or Christianly.

In today's society, the concept of home has disintegrated. Will you allow me to set some ideals? Few of us can achieve all of these ideals, but isn't it good to strive for them? Fortunate indeed is the Toddler who begins life and has it nurtured in a home with the following ideals:

1. A home where both father and mother serve the roles intended. I want to immediately recognize those heroic people who must, as single parents, serve both roles. But I believe that God intended a family to have both husband and wife, father and mother, each serving the role intended.

2. A home where father doesn't dump all of the child care onto the mother, but takes part in the biblically established role of parenting. There are many good books today on the father's role in a Christian home, so I won't linger on the subject, except to say that a father

needs to show spiritual leadership for the home and be a full partner in the parenting process.

3. A home where father and mother express their love to one another openly and role-model before the Toddler and older children the oneness of spirit that should be part of a Christian marriage. Our children have told us through the years that they found enormous security in the obvious and expressed love that Arlie and I have for each other. Fractured husband-wife relationships leave marks of insecurity on a Toddler.

4. A home where both father and mother love the Bible, read it daily with the family, express that love for the Word in numerous ways, and seek to share it with their children in formal and informal ways.

5. A home where it is a delight to grow up. This in itself could make a book. Learn to laugh, especially at yourself. Learn to find some ways each day for you and your Toddler to have fun, to sow the seeds of joy that will keep growing into a full, mature Christian life of joy.

6. A home where parents involve themselves in their children's activities and daily life. In his book *Childhood's Future,* Richard Louv, a newspaper reporter, tells of a nationwide tour that he took to understand the thinking of parents and children. More than anything else, children wanted their parents to spend time with them. They didn't want material things nearly as much as they wanted their parents. There is no substitute for personal time spent with Toddlers.

7. A home where parents and children eat as many meals together as possible and use those times associat-

ed with food to talk, with delight, about God and His Word and His ways. This sounds ideal, but then we are talking about ideals.

8. A home where there is a conscious effort to help Toddlers begin to learn Bible truth, and as they grow older, to build on that truth until as teens they begin to formulate their Christian life view.

9. A home which is a refuge from a hostile society, where the Toddler learns affirmation and affection and can build a healthy self-image.

This is only a taste. You and I could add dozens of other ideals, but that is beyond the space we have in this book.

Chapter Twenty-six

A Toddler's Parents—Appointed by the King

Does parenting sometimes seem a drag? Sometimes it is. I suppose I have never leaped for joy when I had the "privilege" of changing a dirty diaper. Some of you mothers know what I am saying when I speak of "the pits" part of parenting—when two little children are arguing or sassing back or testing you to see how far they can push you. Even precious little Toddlers do that, don't they? Yes, there are times when you'd like to bail out for an hour or a day and then come back for another go at it.

But when we think of it, even changing dirty diapers should be a celebration. I can hear you say, he *must* be kidding. No, I'm really not. Suppose you learned that your child had a severe bowel condition where there would be no dirty diaper until surgery corrected that condition. You would celebrate a dirty diaper when it happened, wouldn't you? I would.

Or suppose your child tore her palate and lost her speech. You would wish desperately you could hear even an argument or a bit of sassing.

Though our work doesn't all seem royal, we parents are appointed by the King of kings for a royal task. We are commissioned by King Jesus to lead His little one, that precious Toddler, into a fuller knowledge of His Word and devotion to Him, to mature into a life of service to Him. Dirty diapers, bottles, laundry, washing dishes, and dozens of other seemingly "unroyal" tasks are all part of the Divine Appointment. They are part of God's plan for a growing Toddler.

This is a chapter to help you celebrate your royal appointment, the highest privilege on earth. There is a trend today of depreciating the role of parenthood, and I grieve for those who miss the joy of it.

I married a lovely girl forty-three years ago so I could spend time with her and share the joys of life with her. Then we had children, five of them, so we could spend time with them in their growing-up process, to guide them and nurture them, and help them grow biblically and spiritually, and while we were doing this, to have fun and build delight. I do not regret one minute I have spent in parenting. I do regret not having more minutes, and hours and days, to spend in that royal appointment.

So what is so royal about being a parent? Let me suggest a few of the royal privileges:

1. You are appointed to the privilege of helping to build a person's life from the Toddler years to the doorstep of the college years. That formative life is in your hands, and the kind of person he or she becomes will depend much on your response to the royal appointment.

2. You are appointed to the privilege of establishing a family legacy for generations to come. This sounds a little heady when you look at your little Toddler, but your little Toddler will become an adult, and will likely have children who will have children and grandchildren, and they in turn will have children and grandchildren.

Would it surprise you to think that your careful shepherding of your little Toddler could ultimately impact generations to come? We are convinced that Arlie's praying grandmother has left her prayer prints on five generations, most of them Christians today and many in career ministry.

3. You are appointed to set the boundaries of happiness in your home, to make it a place of joy or sorrow, victory or defeat.

4. You are appointed to lead lives into the Word of God, to help them understand it and apply it and to accept the Savior and make a reservation to live in the courts of heaven forever.

5. You are appointed to be a faithful steward of the human resources delegated to you by the Creator of the universe, to follow His plans and purposes.

The next time you change a diaper or hold a bottle or wash some clothes or read a story, remember — the King appointed you. You may even want to shout a hallelujah or two.

Chapter Twenty-seven
Are Devotions for Toddlers?

We often think of devotions, or family altar, as the time when we should focus our family on the Word of God and prayer. It is. But I have found many, if not most, Christian parents frustrated because of unrealistic expectations in family devotions. They have set ideals that are too ideal, too unrealistic. When they can't measure up, they want to chuck the whole thing. Devotions don't work, they think.

Having led five children through this whole process into their adult lives, I empathize with these frustrated parents, whether the children are Toddlers or teens.

First, are devotions for Toddlers? There are three answers—yes, yes, and yes. I think you must start your spiritual training from the day a child is born, or even prenatally.

But keep realistic expectations. Don't expect more than can be delivered. Here are a few suggestions for devotions, starting in the Toddler years.

1. Keep devotions within reach of your child. Don't read from Isaiah and expect your Toddler to sit still. I never found a Bible for Toddlers, one I could use in devotions, so I developed one, *The Toddlers Bible.* This was not merely an exercise in writing shorter sentences and using more simple words, but trying to capture the way a Toddler thinks and talks. It is an expression of

Bible events (which is the basis for a Toddler's Bible learning) the way a Toddler expresses things.

2. Try to have devotions at a set time and place each day, such as after dinner but before dishwashing. Or you may prefer the soft minutes just before bedtime. But be flexible because it will not always work that way. While you want to set a habit, you must realize that life today doesn't always fit a mold like that. When your children reach school age they can't always be there, or you can't always do it then. Don't get bent out of shape when this happens. Roll with it. Try it next time.

3. Keep devotions for Toddlers simple and short. You will learn your child's attention span. Don't be surprised if it's two minutes one night and twenty another night. Learn to work with that attention span. Going beyond it is counterproductive.

4. Keep devotions a delight. When you lay a guilt trip or enforce "discipline," or make devotions a pressured time, you lose what you want most to gain, a love for the Word.

5. Remember, devotions are times to meet God through His Word. These are not ultimately times to "teach the Bible." Through your visits in the Word, your child should meet God as a wonderful Friend who wants to help your child live with Him forever, and en route to please Him and serve Him.

6. Keep devotions a family time. It is a special time when families can be bonded. Look for ways to build that family bonding—to bring the family together, not tear the family apart.

7. Role-model your love for the Word and for the

Lord. You will not likely help your child cultivate a greater love for the Lord and His Word than you have. (But someone else may help your child go beyond your "love level for the Lord," to a higher level where that person lives.) So cultivate your own love for the Word and for the Lord first. Then share that love with your Toddler.

You may not even choose to call this time "devotions." The term doesn't matter—Bible time, family time, sunshine time—you choose. The format isn't ordained by God either. But the end result is part of the royal appointment mentioned earlier.

Chapter Twenty-eight
Devotions for Toddlers — Formal or Informal?

If you have Toddlers in your house, you realize that they don't sit still very long. Someone I know tried to imitate the motions of his Toddler. After an hour he was worn out. His Toddler was still going.

"Formal devotions" usually means "sit still while I go through the routine." As a steady diet for long periods of time, that's not for Toddlers, at least not without breaks to let them run around or do something physical.

It probably is good to have a few minutes of a routine. It may be as simple as reading from a book. I have found that it's better to let the Toddler's interest span be the guide, rather than predetermining the length of time I will read. Sometimes I'm surprised to see one of my Toddlers (now grand-Toddlers) leap from my lap almost before I have read a page. Sometimes I'm even more surprised to see one of them sit for a much longer time that I could expect.

By "formal" we mean following a pattern. Reading a Bible book or another book which helps a child learn about God can become a formality — same place, same chair, same time of day, same person reading, and for the Toddler often the same book. That's formal.

Those of you who read to your Toddlers know that they love repetition within a story. *The Toddlers Bedtime Story Book* makes use of repetition in ways that

Toddlers enjoy. That's formality of sorts.

I wouldn't rule out formality in devotions with Toddlers. But I would encourage you to tune your time with a Toddler to her interest span. When it's over, so is your reading time.

But I would also encourage you to develop informal ways to sensitize your Toddler to God and His ways. A walk outside brings all kinds of wonderful signs of the Creator. Talk about them, and the One who made them. Mealtime is a time to reflect on God's provision and His tender loving care.

When you're helping your Toddler get dressed, talk about God's gift of clothing. Remind your Toddler that God and parents team up to bring these things.

You can gently remind your Toddler of God's care in almost everything you do and as you use almost anything you have. Put seasonal pictures on the refrigerator door or a bulletin board or on the door of your child's room. Use them as a springboard to talk about the One who makes pumpkins or leaves or trees or snow or flowers.

Through the years I believe we have helped our children, and now grandchildren, learn more about God informally than formally. If you look for opportunities to talk about God, you'll find them everywhere. But much has been learned in our family in our formal times with God.

Remember, music can be a wonderful aid in helping your Toddler learn about God. If you sing a song such as, "The B-I-B-L-E, yes that's the Book for me," you have a springboard to talk about the Bible as God's

Book and what we learn in it. If you sing "This Little Light of Mine," you can talk about ways we can tell others about our Friend Jesus. What are your favorite songs which you sing with your Toddlers? What can you teach them about God and His Word after you sing each one?

Formal or informal devotions for Toddlers? Both-and, not either-or. Using both instead of one exclusively will also help your Toddler form habits and delights about devotions that will carry through into the older age-levels. The formal-informal teamwork is a good pattern for children of all ages. It's actually a good pattern even for adults.

Always remember to help your Toddler learn something about God or His Word. Devotions are not just fact-learning times, even good facts about the Bible, but so much more.

Chapter Twenty-nine
Building Best Friends Starts at the Toddler Age

Our children are our best friends. I wonder if that's partly because we have always been their best friends.

Best friends love each other and are not afraid to say so. Through the years we have made a point of affirming our love verbally to our children, and have done it often. Our children are grown and married now. But we still remind them of our love. And they remind us of their love for us. More often than not our three daughters sign off of a phone conversation with "love ya."

Best friends like to spend time with each other. Here is a test for you to ask yourself: Do I really like to spend time with my children? Do you? Or would you rather stick in a video and get them off your back? For a short break, that's OK. We all need short breaks, even from people we love. But as a habit?

Best friends enjoy one another's presence. Nearness is a warm fuzzy thing. Nearness is a celebration of "you." The warmth of presence is seen in so many ways, but they all come down to one—I want to be with you whenever I can.

Best friends enjoy doing things together. Through the years we have enjoyed playing games with our children, hiking with our children, going places with our children, and so on. When we went on a trip, if at all possible, the children went with us. When we planned a vacation, we tried to do something that the children would enjoy.

For years I have advised parents, "If you want your children to be with you on the trail when they are twenty-five, you should be on the trail with them when they are five." Habits and traditions are formed through the growing-up years. They are carried out as family rituals as long as time and money permit. If you want a habit or ritual to give you continuity, start it early, in the Toddler years.

Best friends serve one another with gladness. If you have a Toddler, you are learning to serve. But it isn't enough merely to serve. We must serve with gladness. Doing something special for each other is almost a game in our house. Actually serving with gladness should be almost a game — constantly seeing who can outdo the other in doing something nice. It's infectious.

I heard a publisher of a general book company talk about the games that he and his wife played — seeing who could outdo the other in doing something nice for the other. Didn't Jesus tell us "Give and it will be given to you"? (Luke 6:38) As we give to others, so others give to us. That even works with the way we give our lives to our children, starting with Toddlers. The measuring cup with which we pour out our lives to our children may be the same measuring cup with which they will pour out their lives to us in our later years.

Looking back, I believe the greatest reward Arlie and I have received from the parenting process is the assurance that our children are our best friends. While you are helping Toddlers grow, it may be difficult for you to fully comprehend this little child as your best friend someday. But it can happen. And what a delight it is!

Best friends learn how to talk with one another and help each other know what is stirring in their minds and hearts. We will talk more about that in the next chapter.

Is it too much to suggest that we begin a friendship with our child in the mother's womb? I think not. When we talk to that child, sing to that child, and set up beautiful vibes that we hope will register somehow in that unborn child, we start something wonderful. No, an unborn child will not comprehend what you are saying. But something special does happen, a bonding of sorts begins.

Chapter Thirty
Much Time or Quality Time?

Surveys tell us that the average father spends less than one minute per day in quality time with a child. It's rather difficult, wouldn't you say, to build a quality relationship with a minute per day? With the advent of the electronic baby-sitter, the tube, many mothers are spending less quality time with their children too. It's too easy to let the tube do the parenting. With the wretched fare on TV today, what a sorry state of parenting that is.

There is a bit of controversy concerning the time that parents do spend with their children. One side of the controversy measures parental involvement in the number of minutes or hours spent with the child. Others say that quality time is more important than quantity of time. Both are right and both are wrong, I believe.

Quality one-on-one time is vital. We must spend time with each child where we can give undivided attention. For some time each day, your Toddler needs your complete attention as if there were no one else in the world except the Toddler and you. That's quality time. It's quality time especially if you are engaged in that vital life-building process we have been describing in this book, with the Word of God as the conduit between your Toddler as a person and God as a Person, with you as a person leading the process. It is quality time when it is focused time—focused on your Toddler and focused on the process and what it takes to accomplish your goals.

But one minute of quality time doesn't cut it. Neither does one hour of time that goes nowhere. There is a balance of quality one-on-one time in a quantity sufficient to accomplish your goals. How much is that? You must answer that for yourself. I will challenge you, and hope that it isn't a guilt trip, to ask how much time you spend watching TV or playing golf, or doing something else you want to do. If you are spending more time with the tube than you spend building your Toddler's spiritual life, it's time for a personal checkup to see where your priorities are and where the greater eternal benefit is.

Having a specific time to read to your Toddler does help you focus on some quality one-on-one time. Sometimes your reading time is more like one-on-two or one-on-three. I have warm wonderful memories of Arlie each night with the children before their bedtimes. She was reading or singing with animation, and they were giving her their full attention. It is not surprising that they all love to read now as adults.

Having a specific time, such as after dinner at the table, for family devotions also builds a time for quality one-on-one or one-on-more time.

Quality time comes to the forefront with family activities—a trip to the zoo, a picnic, a hike, backyard fun times, travel, etc. When we traveled, we always spent time in the car doing something that was fun—games, Bible memory, or just fun talk. Travel can be a real downer with kids, or it can be just plain fun. It depends on how much quality time you really want to spend with them.

Quality time with your Toddler relates to the previous chapters on personhood. If you have a high regard for your Toddler as a person, you will want to spend time with her. If you don't, you won't. If you have the same regard for your Toddler that God has, you will be hungry to spend quality time with him.

My son Ron spends quality playtime each evening with his three children. It can go from a half hour to an hour. He is a busy executive in a publishing company. I asked him why he does that and he laughed and said, "Because you did it and it was so important to me." Ron also takes each child on a trip occasionally, just one at a time.

Another man I know takes each child to breakfast from time to time. I wish I had thought of that when my children were growing up. What a time to build a talking relationship.

Quality time—yes! Quantity of time—yes! A quantity of quality time—yes and yes! A quantity of quality time that builds a relationship with God—a triple yes!

Chapter Thirty-one
Building Traditions for Toddlers

Traditions help teach Toddlers the Bible, as well as older children. The people of the Bible were saturated with traditions, including numerous feasts and festivals, such as the weekly Sabbath, and many other rituals that bonded their families together.

In our family we have built some of these traditions into family life, and they have become great opportunities for Bible learning. Let me share with you some of our family rituals which from the earliest days of their Toddler years helped our children learn Bible truths:

1. The Sunday dinner. Fortunately our family members live in the area, except for Cindy and her husband. Whenever we can, usually twice or more each month, we gather together after church for a big family dinner. Each family brings something. Each takes part in the cleanup. We eat together, laugh together, talk together. While the cousins, our grandchildren, run off to play together, we adults sit around the table for a while, talking about many things. We play games together, hike together, go outside in good weather to play games with the children, and generally celebrate each other. It is a time for family bonding. It also presents many opportunities to talk together about the things of the Lord and to drop informal insights to the children about God at work among us.

2. The birthday ritual. Whenever a family member (there are eighteen of us now—children, their mates, grandchildren) has a birthday, we celebrate. If the birthday is during the week, the birthday person can expect a call from every other adult family member. The next time we get together for a Sunday dinner, we celebrate that person's birthday with cake and that person's favorite menu. If the birthday boy or girl is a child, he or she will find balloons, lots of them, around the house, with streamers and much attention.

3. The holiday ritual. Holidays bring out the house decorations. Arlie loves to decorate the house. When our children were young and lived with us, they decorated the house seasonally. They clipped seasonal pictures from magazines, especially *Ideals,* which is abundant with seasonal pictures and filed them by seasons in big envelopes. Each seasonal decoration was a reminder of the Creator and His fingerprints and footprints in the world around us. Seasons also suggest menus and cake decorations and special cookies.

Christmas is month-long. It is a big celebration in our house and leads up to the annual ritual where on Christmas Eve I read from Matthew 2 and Luke 2 the real Christmas story. I have done this as far back as I can remember. Christmas also brings out Arlie's favorite cookies, which she bakes in abundance.

Easter at our house includes coloring eggs and hunting for the Easter basket. But mostly it includes a focus on the crucifixion and resurrection of Jesus Christ.

Thanksgiving is also a big dinner festival. We alternate every other year with the parents of our children's mates. But we always have a big turkey and one special tape (originally a record) that brings tears to our children's eyes whenever they hear it. We have played it annually for as long as I can remember.

4. The Turkey Run ritual. Each fall when leaves are in full color, our family takes a long weekend at Turkey Run State Park in Indiana. My mother visited Turkey Run in 1915, shortly after it opened. I was there as a boy. Arlie and I began visiting this beautiful place shortly after we were married. I carried my children on my shoulders when they were too little to walk. It is a family tradition that is as rock-solid as any Jewish festival in Bible times.

Each year we hike the trails together, all of us, and go to the Covered Bridge Festival, an old-fashioned bash on a village courtyard lawn, eat together, and find ways to reflect upon the Lord's goodness.

Rituals help our family, and other families, set up patterns which provide opportunities to talk about the Lord and His Word and to share the truths of the Word together. These are important contexts for the teaching of the Word to Toddlers, and to all ages.

Chapter Thirty-two

All Nature Sings—Learning Truth about God from His Fingerprints

Everywhere we look we see the footprints and fingerprints of the Creator. What a wonderful universe He has made! People have left it scarred, but God's work was good, very good, as we learn in the Creation story.

Have you ever thought how many Bible truths are reinforced in Creation? Have you ever realized how much we learn about the Creator from the creative footprints and fingerprints that He has left on His handiwork? These are truths we can share with our Toddler as we walk together throughout God's Creation.

Let's start with the Bible truth that God's Creation, His work, is good (Genesis 1:31). What God has made is good. But how people have corrupted much of it is *not* good.

Or what about the Bible truth that God is the One who made it all (1:1), or that God made people? (1:27) Another great Bible truth is that God made the seasons (8:22). He also made trees and plants (1:11-12); the sun, moon, and stars (1:14-18); and the animals and birds (1:20-25). And He gave us food to eat (1:29).

How can we coordinate the truths from God's Word with the truths learned in His Creation? We have found it helpful to coordinate them in several ways:

1. Take nature hikes with your Toddler. As you do, talk about the things you see and who made them. Talk

about God's wonderful plan for the universe and His even more wonderful plan for you. Each time you travel, or hike, or go biking, or take a picnic, or whatever you do outside as you interact with Creation, find time to talk about the Creator and His plans and purposes. Make these little talks, not big sermons. Little tastes are better than forced feeding.

2. Hang pictures of Creation in strategic places in your house where you and your Toddler can talk about them. Is it a fall picture with leaves changing color? Perhaps you can remind the Toddler of Genesis 8:22, that God made the seasons and promised that they will always be there as long as the earth remains. This opens the door to talking not only about the seasons, but about God's promises and the way He keeps His promises. As I mentioned in chapter 31, we collected seasonal pictures and stored them by seasons in big envelopes. Our children enjoyed being in charge of hanging these seasonal pictures all over the house.

3. When you go grocery shopping, talk with your Toddler about the God who made all the food she sees, and how abundant it is. Not only that, but she sees that there is a diversity of food. God planned many kinds of food for us. What about the beauty of it? God made different colors and sizes and shapes of food. Isn't that wonderful? God made your eyes so you can see these things. What about the different tastes? Your Toddler can help remind you of the various kinds of taste. God planned for you to taste different tastes. He also planned for you to smell different smells. A trip to the grocery store is also a walk through various scents.

4. When you shop for clothes, you can talk about the way God gives us clothing—from cotton, which is a plant; from wool, which is from sheep; from leather, which is from animal hides; and so on.

5. When you are reading books, look for signs of Creation, things that God has made. Talk about them. This is especially true when you read Bible stories or *The Toddlers Bible.* Look for God's fingerprints, the things He has made, and talk about the things we learn about God from the things He has made. Then as you do this, look for Bible verses that reinforce the great Bible teachings you see expressed in Creation.

Be sure to remind your Toddler that we never worship Creation, but the One who made it. If the things God made are so wonderful, think how much more wonderful God must be.

As the hymn says, "all nature sings," and it does, for it sings songs of the Creator. Oh, yes, be sure to look for signs of His Creation in the hymns of the church too. His fingerprints are everywhere.

Chapter Thirty-three

Teaching Toddlers the Bible —
A Summary of God's Plan

Here is a summary of the God-given plan for teaching Toddlers the Bible, described throughout this book. Follow this simple plan and you *will* teach your Toddlers the Bible. Or, more properly, you *will* help your Toddlers learn Bible.

1. Recognize the stages of growth from birth through age 18, when your child will likely "leave the nest" and your direct supervision. Recognize the boundaries of the Toddler growth stage.

2. Capture the essence of what childhood is and why each stage of childhood is so important. Determine that you will not knowingly let your child miss important stages of childhood or rush through them. Look at childhood for your child as something wonderful that God created — a divinely planned pattern which you can follow with your child.

3. Identify those goals of personal Christian growth which you hope your child will accomplish by the time he or she leaves home. Identify which portion of those goals may be met during the Toddler years.

4. Identify the doctrines or beliefs which you hope your child will learn as part of his or her Christian life view by the time your child leaves home. Identify which of these may be learned during the Toddler years.

5. Identify the character values which you hope your

117

child will have claimed as his or her own by the time your child leaves home. Recognize that Christian character is what a person becomes as a result of what he or she believes (Christian life view). Identify which character values may be learned during the Toddler years.

6. Recognize that your child will develop a solid Christian life view, or belief system, through an understanding and application of the life-changing truths of the Word of God. Recognize also that he or she will develop a strong Christian character if he follows that Christian life view. Recognize further that Christian conduct is the practical expression of Christian character.

7. Recognize those first three years of your child's life as the most important three years of all life. Don't talk yourself into the idea that your child is "just a little child" and doesn't need as much of your time and effort as an older child would. Start at birth, or even before, interacting with your child and helping your child develop the way he or she should.

8. Set "delight" as the "software program" that drives all Bible study that you do with your child. Delight in the Word and in the Lord should begin during the earliest years of Bible learning.

9. Recognize that the life-changing truths of the Word of God are the hope for your child in a darkening society. Without those truths shaping your child, the future is not bright. With them, your child can stand against the very gates of hell.

10. Determine that the process of helping your child learn, understand, and apply those life-changing truths

from the Word, with delight, is the most important work that you as parent or teacher can do.

11. Determine that this process will take precedence over all others. Set child development—helping your child develop that Christian life view and thence Christian character—as the highest priority of your parenting or teaching. Turn off the tube! Turn on your child to the joy of learning, especially learning the truths of the Word. Read! Sing! Involve yourself with your child!

12. Whatever you teach, or help your child to learn, of the life-changing truths of the Word, first role-model them in your own life. Your role-modeling will transcend your other teaching. Part of that role-modeling is providing a warm, wonderful home environment which is a refuge.

Your Toddler will thank you forever if you follow this simple plan. And you will forever be grateful that you have teamed up with God to build a life that will honor Him, and you.

Chapter Thirty-four

A Dozen Tips—Teaching Toddlers the Bible

We have talked about these throughout this book. But it is time to summarize a dozen of them here for easy access.

1. Read a good Toddler's Bible regularly. I couldn't find one, so I developed one, called *The Toddlers Bible.* Talk with your Toddler about what you have read. Ask questions.

2. Read other good books which are designed for your Toddler and will share the truths of the Word with him or her.

3. Sing songs that reflect Bible truths, songs your Toddler will enjoy. The old standby, "Jesus Loves Me" is still one of the best. It is a doctrinal foundation stone for your Toddler. So is "The B-I-B-L-E." Ask in a Christian bookstore for a book of Christian songs and choruses for little children.

4. Try Bible memory, but just parts of Bible verses. Whole verses are usually too complex for Toddlers. Choose verses which communicate simple truths that your Toddler can grasp.

5. Choose a fixed time to read or sing or have devotions in some other way with your Toddler. When you can't do it, don't feel pangs of guilt. Try it next time. Strive for a pattern, but don't blow a fuse when you can't.

6. Through all you do, keep a spirit of delight, DE-LIGHT, DELIGHT. When learning the Word becomes a burden, you turn off your Toddler.

7. Talk about God and His Word and the truths of His Word in everyday life. Talk about them on hikes, while traveling in a car, or any other time you have alone with your Toddler. Use "down time," such as driving with your child to the grocery store, as a time to share a wonderful idea about God and His Word.

8. Let pictures kick off a talk about God or something from His Word. Bring them to devotions. Put them on the fridge. Seasonal pictures speak of His Creation, and thus point children to Him.

9. Associate Bible time with a special time of the day, such as mealtime or bedtime. This puts a warm hug around this special time.

10. Involve your Toddler in your family talk. It's easy to make dinner time, for example, a time to review all the problems at the office. Can you find another time apart from your Toddler to do this? Include the whole family in dinner talk, and bring God and the truths of His Word into that conversation softly, without hitting your Toddler over the head with them.

11. Find Christian activities that are for Toddlers that teach the truths of the Word. Do them frequently.

12. Pray earnestly that the truths of God's Word will find root in your Toddler's heart and mind. Expect that these truths are but simple seeds of truth sown. The fruit will come later. Expect great things from God and He will pour them abundantly into your life as you faithfully serve your role as parent and teacher.

A Pre-primer of Bible Doctrines

Seeds Sown—
Doctrines Your Toddler Will Learn in
The Toddlers Bible

The Toddlers Bible has a built-in program of Bible doctrines for Toddlers. It is a pre-primer of doctrine, sowing the early seeds of truth that grow later into a full Christian life view. This is not a complete doctrinal program for Toddlers, only those that are taught in *The Toddlers Bible*.

God Gives Us Good Things

God gives good gifts   **48–51**
God gives us our homes **128–31**
God makes us strong   **140–43**
God gives us good food **104–7,**
124–27, 176–79, 308–11
God gives children to parents **78**
God gives us all we need   **107**
God gives us many things **168–71**

God Has Special Plans for Us

God has special plans for us **42**

God Helps Us

God helps us when we
ask   **156–59**

God helps us do His
work   **84–87, 168–71**
God helps us when we obey
Him   **132–35**
God helps a few people do
big things   **136–39**
God helps us do good
things   **140–43**
God helps us when we
need Him   **100–103**
God helps His helpers **188–91**
When God promises to
help us, He will do it   **130**

God Is a Wonderful God

God is wonderful   **19**
God is everywhere   **216–19**

122

123

A Pre-primer of Character Values

Seeds sown —
Christian Character Development

Tiny Seeds of Values Will Be Sown
in Your Toddler As You Use *The Toddlers Bible*

Your Toddler will learn to be:

Brave

David was brave when he
fought Goliath. We are braver
when God helps us.   **156–59**

Paul was brave. He even told a
king about Jesus.   **404–7**

Faithful

Daniel was faithful to God. He
would not eat the wrong food.
We should be faithful to God
and not do what is wrong.
208–11

Forgiving

A father forgave his runaway
boy. We should forgive people
who ask us.   **328–31**

Friendly

Jonathan and David did good
things for each other. We do
good things for our best
friends.   **160–63**

Saul needed a friend. Barnabas
became his friend. We should
help people who need a friend.
392–95

Giving

People gave happily to build the
tabernacle. Giving to God
makes us happy.   **116–19**

People gave money to fix God's
house. We should give to take
care of God's house.   **192–95**

Wise men gave their best gifts

to Baby Jesus. We should give our best to Jesus. **232–35**

A poor woman gave her best. We should give our best. **356–59**

Good

God and Jacob promised to do good things for each other. God has promised to do good to us. We should promise to do good things for God. **56–59**

Helpful

Adam and Eve helped to care for God's world. We should help God care for His world. **18**

Jacob helped Rachel take care of her sheep. We should help others when they need us. **60–63**

David asked God to help. That's why he beat Goliath. God helps us when we ask. **156–59**

God sent Elijah to help a poor woman. We should help when God wants us to. **180–83**

Elisha was God's helper. We should be God's helpers. **188–91**

Some men helped Nehemiah build walls. We should help God's helpers. **196–99**

Joseph and Mary helped care for Baby Jesus. We should help Jesus too. **236–39**

Jesus' friends helped Him do His work. We should help Jesus do His work. **272–75**

Matthew helped Jesus do His work. We should help Jesus do His work. **280–83**

Jesus asked 12 men to be His helpers. We can be Jesus' helpers too. **284–87**

A blind man asked Jesus for help. Jesus helped him. Jesus will help us when we ask. **344–47**

Saul became Jesus' helper. We should be Jesus' helpers. **388–91**

Dorcas was a good helper. We should help others as Dorcas did. **396–99**

Timothy's mother helped him love God's Word. We should help others love God's Word. **412–15**

Honest

Jacob cheated his brother. We should never cheat anyone. **44–47**

Humble

God punished proud people who built a tower. God may punish us if we get proud. **32–35**

Kind

Ruth was kind to Naomi. We should be kind to our families. **144–47**

King David was kind to Mephibosheth. We should be kind to those who have less. **164–67**

Loving

Joseph's brothers hated him and sold him. We should love our family. Hating makes us do bad things. **64–67**

Job kept loving God, even when bad things happened. We should keep loving God, even when bad things happen. **204–7**

Jesus loves us as a shepherd loves his sheep. We should love Jesus. **316–19**

Jesus loves us. He wants to save us. We should love Jesus and follow Him. **324–27**

Jesus loves children. We should love children. **340–43**

Jesus loves us. He even died for us. We should love Jesus and His friends. **368–71**

Obedient

Adam and Eve disobeyed God. We should obey God. **20–23**

Noah obeyed God because he loved God. If we love God, we will obey Him. **24–27**

Noah helped God take care of him by obeying. We help God take care of us by obeying. **28–31**

Joshua obeyed God. God helped him win. God helps us when we obey Him. **132–35**

Gideon obeyed God. God helped him win. God helps us when we obey Him. **136–39**

Jonah learned to obey God in a big fish. Obey God, even when you don't want to. **216–19**

Jesus obeyed God, not Satan. We should obey God. **256–59**

A storm obeyed Jesus. We should obey Jesus. **300–303**

Wind and waves obeyed Jesus. We should obey Jesus. **312–15**

Patient

When bad things happened, Job was patient. Be patient, even if bad things happen. **204–7**

Peaceful

Isaac gave up his wells rather than fight. God gave him good things for doing this. God gives us good things when we are peaceful. **48–51**

Persevering

Nehemiah kept building the walls, no matter what happened. Keep doing what God wants. Don't stop for anything. **196–99**

Prayerful

Noah thanked God for taking care of him and his family. We should thank God for taking care of us and our family. **28–31**

Abraham thanked God for a special son. We should thank God for special gifts. **36–39**

Isaac and Rebekah asked God for a baby. When we need something special, we may ask God for it. **40–43**

Jacob and God promised to do good things for each other. God has promised us good things. We should promise to do good things for Him. **56–59**

Moses prayed for God to help his people. God helped them. God listens to our prayers and answers them. **84–87**

Samuel listened when God talked to him. We should listen to God's Word. **148–51**

King Solomon prayed for God to make him wise. We should ask God for the right gifts. **168–71**

Solomon prayed at God's house. We should pray at God's house. **175**

Daniel kept praying even when he could get hurt. Nothing should keep us from praying. **212–15**

Mary talked with Jesus. He said that was very important. Talking with Jesus is more important than working. **320–23**

Jesus prayed. We should pray. **364–67**

Sharing

A man and woman shared their house and food with Elisha. We should share good things with God's helpers. **188–91**

A boy shared His lunch with Jesus. He shared it with 5,000. We should share our best with Jesus. He will use it well. **308–11**

Some women shared the Good News about Jesus. We should share His Good News with others. **374–77**

Philip shared the Good News with an Ethiopian. We should

share Jesus' Good News with
others. 384–87

Thankful

Noah thanked God for taking
care of him and his family. We
should thank God for taking
care of our family. 28–31

Abraham and Sarah thanked
God for their baby. We should
thank God for special
gifts. 36–39

Moses thanked God for helping
him and his people. We should
thank God for His help. 92–95

Elijah thanked God for food.
We should thank God for
food. 176–79

A man and woman were thank-
ful that Elisha was God's helper.
We should thank God for His
helpers. 188–91

One man thanked Jesus, but
nine did not. We should
remember to thank Jesus for
helping us. 336–39

Trusting

Moses trusted God to help his
people cross a sea. We should
trust God for wonderful
things. 100–103

Moses trusted God to send
food in the desert. We should
trust God for food every
day. 104–7

People who did not trust God
were sad. We are sad when we
do not trust God. 128–31

Job kept trusting God when bad
things happened. We should
keep trusting God, even if bad
things happen. 204–7

Truthful

Jacob lied to his father. We
should never lie. 52–55

Someone lied about Joseph. He
had to go to jail. When we lie
about someone we may hurt
that person. 68–71